THE NATURE CHRONICLES PRIZE
-1-

WINNING ENTRIES

WITH AN INTRODUCTION BY
KATHRYN AALTO

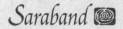

Saraband

Published by Saraband
3 Clairmont Gardens,
Glasgow, G3 7LW

www.saraband.net

*Published in association with
the Prudence Scott Charitable Trust*

ISBN: 9781913393687

Printed and bound in Great Britain by Clays Ltd, Elcograf S.p.A.

1 3 5 7 9 10 8 6 4 2

CONTENTS

CONTENTS

KATHRYN AALTO

INTRODUCTION

The invitation tasted like a peach on a hot summer day. Would I like to be part of a new, biennial, international literary award and spend a weekend in Windermere, Cumbria, with others, judging new nature writing?

Juicy offers such as this are readily accepted.

And so, over several months, we five judges – ecopoet and academic Elizabeth-Jane Burnett, zoology professor Matthew Cobb, publisher Sara Hunt, critic and bookseller Will Smith, and myself, a writer, teacher, and historian – brought our diverse backgrounds to assess and applaud, sort and shortlist, the anonymous submissions selected by readers for this inaugural prize.

Created in memory of Prudence Scott, a nature diarist and long-time resident of Windermere, the aim of The Nature Chronicles Prize is 'to find engaging, unique, essay-length non-fiction that responds to the time we are in and the world as it is, challenging established notions of nature writing where necessary.' The winner receives £10,000 and five runners up £1,000 each. These six entries are the result of a judging process that was collective and individualistic, methodical and intuitive.

Upon gathering in Windermere this past summer, the judges were delighted, and maybe a little relieved, to discover that there was significant overlap in our individual shortlist choices. Though each of us may have lost an essay that we felt strongly about, we listened to and accepted others' points of view. These 'losses' are an inevitable part of such a process, as we were judging both the literary quality *and* the content (the ideas, scope and relevance to prize criteria). We saw that although sometimes our views on the relative strengths of individual essays might not align, our collective desire for consistent content and quality always did.

We first extend our warm congratulations to Nicola Pitchford, Winner of the 2022 Nature Chronicles Prize.

Her essay 'A Parable for Arable Land' is a richly layered reading experience. It is framed by a personal story, about her late father, which she dilates to ask a universal question, 'What does it mean to do good in the world?' 'Perhaps by reading the story of the land,' Pitchford writes, 'I can write into that larger narrative – and by doing so, I might find a way in, to take up the nascent work of restitution that was cut short when his life ended.' Pitchford's piece was widely admired by the judges for its well-crafted narrative nonfiction techniques and for her use of an engaging first-person presence that eschews solipsism. There was a strong sense of place across time and space, and insights into a facet of modern landscape history. We admired its pleasing circular structure and the way this shape reflected the legacy of her father's work. Not only did 'A Parable of Arable Land' make us *think* deeply, but we had the sense that Prudence Scott might also have chosen it.

We would also like to congratulate the other shortlisted writers and share some of their particularly noteworthy elements.

'The Flight of the Goshawk' by Ben Crane was a compelling runner up. This unflinching essay has a hot, wild breath. Crane writes a brisk, braided narrative – self-portrait of himself as a falconer, brief histories of epidemics, heart-pumping scenes of hunting – and in doing so, he transports readers. We soar over fields and blackthorn hedges. We feel the COVID-19 virus careening through his own inner landscapes. We begin to understand what it must be like to inhabit other ways of being in the natural world. 'Out there in the landscape, out flying, is to collapse any boundaries between myself and the natural world,' Crane writes with admirable vulnerability, 'to feel no sense of enclosure, experience no demarcated rules. I am in the now; I become uncoiled, all my senses receptive to the humming vibration between myself, the hawk, the dog, the earth, air, blood, and mud. I feel a definite transformation into the best I can be. This sophisticated and complicated sensation is the primary inspiration for writing, self-expression, self-reflection, and self-knowledge. In this context nature is a guiding light, a moral focal point, the only *true* way of measuring myself.'

Our gaze turns from the skies to the ground at our feet in Jenny Chamarette's 'Q is for Garden'. This essay opens with a small snail shell falling from a pruned branch onto the pages of an open book. We watch as a tiny hermaphrodite snail slides across the pages, opening a refreshing essay on queerness, sexuality, and love, coupled with the complex reproductive sexualities of snails.

We felt Laura Coleman's 'The Fence' was so stylishly written that it could have been fiction. Confident use of dialogue and well-written characters drop readers into scenes to create memorable portraits of people living in a community on a Hebridean island. This is an essay about boundaries and relationships written in sharp and vivid imagery.

In contrast to this slow life is the almost sci-fi sense of unreality in 'None of This Should Be Here', by Joanna Pocock. This gritty essay is about displacement, loss, and overconsumption in the desert ecosystem of Las Vegas. After personal tragedies,

Pocock departs Las Vegas on a Greyhound bus, she herself looks into the sky – 'Life had conspired to bring me to a patch of desert under a shroud of black sky' – and finds solace in knowing what *does* belong.

We felt 'City of Covid Trees' by Neha Sinha brought a vital global perspective, putting the pandemic at the heart of the story and graphically revealing the different ways it was experienced. Experiencing COVID-19, she draws strengths from trees in India – the Neem and the Palash. 'The tree stood like a God, radiating with orange flowers. A plant God – one that did not need the appreciation of human worshippers, one that flowered and fruited without a built shrine.'

I would also like to say a few words about essays that were close, but ultimately did not make the shortlist.

'The Garden' by Nicola Healey was eloquently championed on grounds of pushing against the ableism so often seen in nature writing and other genres. We also felt that it celebrated the importance of small urban green spaces during lockdown. The passages about anosmia, the partial or full loss of smell, were vital and interesting, and the standard of writing was excellent.

A beautiful sense of isolation and a love letter to remote rural life was evoked in 'The Settling Snow' by Patrick Laurie. We appreciated its sense of place

INTRODUCTION

– that layer of memories, history, and emotions covering a physical landscape with invisible strata – and the way place knowledge passed through generations. The essay is filled with croaking ravens, bleating lambs, and snowy fields as well as one memorable scene of a screaming bull. Writing of his grandfather, 'I saw the intimacy of his relationship and wanted it for myself, because the line between his person and his place was indistinguishable.'

Too often in nature writing, humour is excluded, perhaps for fear of laughing at a funeral as seas rise, biodiversity plummets, and temperatures climb. This is understandable. However, we appreciated the way compelling perspectives of managing wildlife were balanced with occasional comedic moments in 'Ape Town' by Tim Dee, including a 'baboon hotline' and vivid domestic scenes. We valued the way the essay highlighted deleterious human-centric perspectives which seem to forget that it is we humans who have altered the territory and displaced the animals that the human community – the interlopers – now view as 'a nuisance'.

In 'The Butter Bump' by David Higgins, we appreciated the insights into the bittern, especially the imaginative linguistic and naming history of this bird through time – billy bellow, *boeuf de marais*, bog drum, butter bump, French heron. The first-person narrative is also vulnerable. It invites readers to appreciate moments of transcendence with greater-than-human life: 'No doubt my sometimes obsessive listing/collecting of species is yet another fruitless hedge against death, but birdwatching has made me feel connected to the more-than-human world for the first time since I was a young child.' We valued the meditation on common land and belonging that was 'The Unbounded Land' by Helen Baczkowska. We liked the language in Kerry Andrew's 'The Story Fox', comparing how foxes are depicted in different cultural traditions, but always as some form of trickster figure.

The judges enjoyed reading submissions about marine life. We appreciated the symbolism of the jellyfish as a compass in 'Other Blooms' by Saskia McCracken. In 'We Grieve Only for What We Know', by Anna Selby, we were struck by the passage: 'For me, the best classrooms and lessons are not in rooms and not only factual, but felt and experienced: what it feels like to turn my face up and watch terns bullet through the surface toward me, watching the last upturn of their arcs, the water bubbling and boiling around them; or to look a sea turtle in the eye, so close I see myself reflected in her iris, and then to have this ancient creature swim vertically up around my body; or when a species of fish I've never seen before drips down in front of my goggles; and most of all, what it is to be in

INTRODUCTION

a borderless space that connects every part of our planet. I feel part rather than apart, as if I could go everywhere.'

We hope the essays in this inaugural Nature Chronicles Prize anthology transport you and inspire you to feel a part of something bigger.

KATHRYN AALTO
September 2022

THE WINNING ESSAY

NICOLA PITCHFORD

A PARABLE OF ARABLE LAND

Two miles east of here, where the road past our last-of-the-suburbs neighbourhood peters out into a municipal park, wetlands, and eventually the edge of San Pablo Bay, there used to be a nuclear missile emplacement. When, over recent years, things have seemed particularly dark in the world, it gives me some comfort to think about that. From the 1950s through the '70s, the potential for apocalypse lurked there in bunkers at the end of our road, ready to defend San Francisco against Soviet bombers. And all that remains of the site now is a few cracked concrete slabs, bleached by sunlight, on a low scrubby hillock overlooking a skate park on one side, a golf course on the other. Beyond, the wide, light-reflecting plane of silver water. It could be that this hill was originally one of the Native American (Coast Miwok) burial mounds that are scattered around the area.

It's a strange and unglamorous strip of land out there at the bay's edge, cut off from the affluent towns along the other side of the north–south freeway and not much frequented – a grab-bag of all the non-residential uses America can think of for flat, marshy land the military no longer wants: a commuter railway, a small airfield, a sewage treatment plant. At one edge, a field of solar panels, interspersed with flowering weeds; on another, a sprawl of deserted metal huts looped by razor-wire fencing that has housed a minimum-security prison and a residential substance-abuse center. For me, however, the no-man's land at the edge of the bay also holds a promise of personal meaning, of a story I need to understand. It's my own small story of what it would mean to *live well with the land*, something we desperately need to know now, none more so than those of us in the resource-gobbling US. Trying to answer that question entangles me in the story of my long-dead father and his work.

Not all the land has been left to randomness and scrub; in parts, gestures of restoration are also evident. Just beyond the great sewage tubs, churned 24/7 by slow machinery, is a destination that's a poorly kept secret among the grey-haired, outdoorsy types over-represented in our local demographic: a series of wastewater ponds encircled by gravel paths, admirably transformed in recent years into a refuge for water birds. Photographers and binoculared birdwatchers gather here under the open sky, focusing intently on pelicans, sandpipers, rare clapper rails, a hundred varieties of waterfowl, and the raptors and corvids that monitor the low surrounding land. At dusk I have also seen jack-rabbits here, coyotes, deer, a family of skunks, and once – magically – a pair of otters.

But the wildlife isn't the only reason I come; I like to say hello to a faint sign of my father, written on the land. Where the very last of the solid ground again turns vague and unregarded are three scruffy fields in the shape of faded circles, separated by earthen dikes from the pickleweed flats at the saltwater's edge. They seem neglected, given over to dockweed and wild mustard, although the lateral bridges of irrigation systems still span the once-cultivated discs, their central pumps protected by wire-mesh fences. Looking at the fields on Google Earth, their circular shape is still clear. Along their margins run tangled hedges of bramble, willow, leggy fennel, coyote brush, and the occasional stunted date palm. Huge northern harriers hover low, their white-based tails fanned out. These fields are the only example of center-pivot irrigation I know of in the county – and wherever I see circular fields, from an airplane window or on foot, I see an indirect message for me, no more than the landscape's subtle wink.

I grew up thinking my father invented center-pivot irrigation (or *centre*-pivot, as I knew it then), although I've since learned it was created by a Midwestern farmer in the 1940s. To this day

A PARABLE OF ARABLE LAND

I don't understand exactly what the innovation was by which Dad significantly improved on the original technology, but I know there was a type of apparatus that he perfected, which proved particularly popular in the Soviet-bloc countries (he worked on projects in Romania, Bulgaria, Hungary, Yugoslavia) and in Soviet satellites in what was confidently called *the underdeveloped world*. Over his desk at home, in England and later in California and Oregon, hung a framed cartoon drawn by a Dutch friend of his; it showed a group of smugly grinning camels, hitched to a center-pivot irrigation apparatus in the middle of a blank desert, slowly rotating it around a circle of alfalfa that they are also munching as they go. To me, that eccentric and mystifying image conjured much: the glamorous internationalism of his life during the extended periods when he was gone from home (an exoticism embedded even in the word 'alfalfa', alien then to our wheat-growing region); his cleverness with adapting technologies to unfamiliar environments; and the sense of amusement with which he approached his work and most other things. It intrigued me, offering a cryptic connection with parts of his world that I could not know.

You've probably seen the green crop circles characteristic of center-pivot irrigation, if you live anywhere but the world's wettest or most forested areas. An overhead metal gantry, anchored to a central well and carrying sprinklers along its length, rotates on wheeled supports, resulting in a watered circle. Some of these circles are so broad in radius, they stand out even in images of the landscape taken from space. The popularity of this system derives from its capacity to provide economical, uniform watering despite uneven ground or tall crops, without the need to sacrifice land to channels dug between rows or to manually move equipment regularly. It was one of the most influential agricultural technologies of the twentieth century.

I grew up in its shadow. Not literally, as my childhood was spent in a green and rainy place thousands of miles from the desert ecosystem where I now live. But thanks to my father's work, the course of my early life, arguably my whole life, was shaped by advances in irrigation technology – and beyond that, by late-twentieth-century changes in how the richer nations think about water itself. In a way, the history of the no-man's land at the edge of the bay echoes the trajectory of my father's career: from Cold War nuclear defense, to large-scale agricultural irrigation, to reclamation and restoration.

Perhaps by reading the story of the land, I can write him into that larger narrative – and by doing so, I might find a way in, to take up the nascent work of restitution that was cut short when his life ended. For many years, I thought him perfect – a saint. From the time I was ten years old until my departure for college, he and I were an inseparable team: a closed circle, attuned to one another to the exclusion of others. I was his special girl. It took a long time for me to see the harm he also did, first on the personal scale of family, and later, within the larger scope of a question he himself taught me to ask: *what does it mean to do good in the world?* In the conversations taking place now in our damaged, imperiled time of climate crisis, it is easier to see the dark falsity of the evangelical technological optimism that opened the world to him as a youth, and of the post-imperial confidence accompanying it – the assumption not only that nature could be harnessed and possessed, but also that it should be.

Dad was a hydrological engineer, an inventor, an oddball. He taught me early on that if you're clever enough, cheerful enough, and strange enough, people will leave you to yourself, give you space to carve your own channel. There wasn't a lot of space where he grew up, at the just-respectable edge of a soot-blackened northern English town in wartime. There, the only water was a charmless beck in a damp, wooded cutting known by locals as The Dingle; by the time I came along in the 1960s, there was always a discarded child's bicycle in the tangled undergrowth along its banks or a broken chair, and oil-slick rainbows glazed its sluggish surface. He sought water elsewhere, won swimming medals in school, and when he owned his first car headed straight to the Lake District or to the Scottish coast to scuba dive. He was even part of the diving team that tried to recover Donald Campbell's *Bluebird* – and Campbell's body – from the depths of Coniston Water, after the ill-starred 1967 attempt on the world water-speed record. And with a kind of inevitability, as a young engineer he soon moved from his first job in aircraft hydraulics to become a designer of submarines, developing propulsion systems for Britain's nuclear fleet – the missile-bearing Polaris. We lived by the coast, with the grand, national heritage of Cumbria and the Lakes at our back.

But there is, as Peter O'Toole's T. E. Lawrence says in *Lawrence of Arabia*, a kind of Englishman who never feels at home in his own 'fat country' of green fields and ponderously grazing cattle; in my father's quest for space he also became one of those strange Englishmen who falls in love with the desert. I don't know the extent to which moral concerns led him to leave the Military–Industrial Complex, as I learned much later to call it. I know he had qualms, although he spoke little about them. And they did not go so deep that he could agree with me when, as a university student in England some fifteen years later, I took part in a mass anti-nuclear 'die-in' protest, lying down on the damp tarmac of the same shipyard where he had once worked. But whatever the reason, he turned his inventive talents toward a different twentieth-century challenge – that of feeding a rapidly growing world. At the time, that meant urgently bringing more land under cultivation, making deserts bloom and yield. The call, for any clever 'water man', was to create innovations in large-scale delivery: pumps and sprinklers. And thus he fell from the ethical frying pan into the fire – the burning fire of Lawrence's Sahara; or more accurately, the Sahara of General Muammar al-Qaddafi.

In the late 1960s and early '70s, Qaddafi's Kufra Oasis Project was the wildly ambitious dreamchild of a despot in the making, the would-be champion of the Non-Aligned Nations. It was to be the cornerstone of food self-sufficiency for Libya, and would stand as a symbol, to Qaddafi's own people and the rest of the world, of the limitless transformative power of Arab ingenuity and scientific acumen – an assertion of continuity between the ancient tradition of the original inventors of mathematics and engineering, and the twentieth-century world of technology and development to which the global North attempted to lay exclusive claim. What spectacle could equal the stunning magic of creating a lush, green, fruitful landscape in the driest, most inhospitable place on earth? What could send a more defiant message than to transform the small natural oasis at al-Kufra – claimed by invaders and colonizers from the Ottomans to the Italians, and more recently central to the North African campaign of World War II – into a peaceable pastoral idyll where the nation could turn for nourishment? Fed by wells tapping ancient aquifers, tens of thousands of hectares of verdant circles would deliver grain and sheep to the coastal cities.

By that time, center-pivot technology had already proven its ability to wrest fertility and abundance from land blighted by drought, dust, and despair: the Great Plains of the United States. Indeed, the two images I remember from our first flight to America, years later, are my prolonged intimacy with the 'sick bag' and Dad calling me out of that humiliation to look down from the window at the great flat quilt of the Midwest, dotted everywhere with clusters of dark green circles. The endless fertility of America's Breadbasket lay below us, and to my confusion I saw that this whole vast, new, and alien country had already been claimed by my father's signature.

The little I know about the contributions he made to facilitating the spread of center-pivot irrigation consists of the fact that he specialized in converting gritty, sandy trickles of water into clean, high-pressure distribution. He won patents for inventions that somehow made the great structures more versatile, resilient, and efficient – that made them more practical for places like the Sahara Desert.

The camp at Kufra where the foreign engineers and agricultural specialists lived was an international village: Dutch, Germans, French, Canadians, Britons, Egyptians, Indians, Australians; and Libyan advisors and workers. Tents and huts stretched out at the great desert's constantly mobile edge. Generators hummed continually, through scorching days and freezing nights. There was a certain amount of multilingual camaraderie, easier for polyglots like my father, who was one of the few Europeans to learn Arabic. (When I brought him his coffee, he always said '*shukran habiba*', and it amused him to call me 'Wahad', which he said could mean not only 'one' but also 'big thing' or 'you there!', although I have not met an Arabic speaker who recognizes the latter usage.) But boredom was endemic. There was nothing to do but work. He told me about one German, a recovering alcoholic confined to this dry (in both senses) place; after increasingly frequent incidents in which bottles of aftershave went missing, the others woke one morning to learn the German had been sent to Tripoli. I was never entirely sure whether he had fallen ill from drinking cologne or been banished for violating cultural standards. It got worse, for some; my father made only passing reference to the man who hanged himself.

The men from wealthier countries (they were all men) must have been misfits, to a certain extent – for whom a sense of adventure, or the love of scientific innovation, or both, were enough to justify months at a time in the desert, away from families and home. It was long before cell phones and Internet. I don't remember my mother ever getting letters.

My father loved it there. He talked about the extreme heat and cold, but also the golden-red sand, the simplicity and scale of the great clean desert, the wind that sculpted the dunes into gentle ripples like the scales of some enormous fish, the movement of light across the vast sky. The camels, he said, all shared an epic halitosis that they inflicted on their handlers in revenge for their servitude. He admired the self-containment of the Zuwayya Bedouin, although what interactions they may have had, I do not know.

*

'Only two kinds of creature get fun in the desert: Bedouins and gods,' Claude Rains as the British ambassador tells T. E. Lawrence. 'You are neither.'

21

A PARABLE OF ARABLE LAND

Lawrence's fellow soldiers and officers see the desert-lover as an eccentric and a 'clown'; later, they speculate that he has 'gone native'. But Prince Faisal – played in shameful brownface by Alec Guinness – immediately recognizes the more sinister side of Lawrence's strange passion: it aligns rather conveniently with his home nation's colonial ambitions, despite his overt embrace of Arab nationalism. 'The English,' Faisal drily observes, 'have a great hunger for desolate places.'

Lawrence's love of the desert is itself a kind of brownface. To the British, it looks Arab, or as they imagine Arabs to be; but in fact, it is profoundly characteristic of British imperialism. 'I think you are another of these desert-loving English,' Faisal/Guinness tells Lawrence in a moment heavy with metatextual irony. 'No Arab loves the desert. We love water and green trees.'

*

Sometimes, in their boredom, the foreigners at Kufra ventured into the dunes at night, lamp-hunting in Jeeps for jerboas, desert rats. It was innocent silliness. Stunning the creatures with their headlights as they bounced across the uneven sand, they would all pile out, shouting and jostling, and compete to catch a jerboa between their hands before the poor thing came fully to it senses and leapt away on 90-degree back legs. It was like primitive rugby, played without rules, with a tiny and fragile ball that could move at great speed to evade the players. Hearing about it worried me, as I thought of my own beloved pet gerbil and her wee bright eyes. Once, a victorious player held aloft his cupped hands in the Jeep's headlight beams, ultrafine sand leaking from between his fingers to dance in the disturbed air, and opened them to display his trophy – only to find the tiny thing had died of fear. After that, my father said, none of them wanted to go hunting for a while. They had meant no harm.

The Kufra Project was a disaster. I've since learned that it is taken as an emblematic example, in development circles, of the unsustainable squandering of natural and financial resources. I don't know if they suspected it at the time; I always had the sense Dad was proud of his work there, of contributing to the conjuring up of abundance. But by the end of the 1970s, the natural lake at al-Kufra had already run dry. (My father had moved on by then.) By the turn of the millennium, it was widely recognized that the massive Nubian Aquifer supplying Kufra's magic – a store of buried fossil water as much as a million years old, beneath much of Egypt and Libya, up to the Mediterranean – was receding at a horrifying rate that far exceeded any possible replenishment. Dr Mansour El-Kikhia, a

A PARABLE OF ARABLE LAND

Libyan exile and political scientist once mooted as a possible replacement for Qaddafi, offers a concise, damning verdict on Qaddafi's desert dreams: 'Spending was thought to be the answer to all of Libya's agricultural problems. The resulting waste is perhaps best exemplified by the Kufra Agricultural Project, *a classic example of an attempt at agricultural independence gone wrong.*' The foreign expertise was soon withdrawn; the great artificial oasis was nothing but a mirage.

*

Here in California, we have our own aquifer problems. Along Interstate 5, the dreary north–south freeway where travelers between Los Angeles and San Francisco grow numb with the monotony of truck traffic, flat fields stretching to every horizon, and a smoggy haze that tastes of manure, an increasing number of handmade signs and billboards appear along the roadside with ominous warnings invoking the words, 'Dust Bowl'. Underground water is being depleted at such a rate that in places the ground is sinking by two feet a year. While repeated recent droughts have contributed to an alarming acceleration, the crisis has been a long time coming. Perhaps it began at the very moment when farmer Frank Zybach invented the center pivot and helped restore the Midwest to life after the original Dust

Bowl, launching a great ironic circle of redemption and depletion that now threatens that region too. 'Center pivot technology epitomizes much of what it is to be an American,' commented a recent article in *Smithsonian Magazine*: 'technological triumph..., ingenuity and drive, but also unchecked resource use and ever-increasing scale.'

My father answered that call of American potential. In his case, it came in the form of a recruiting approach from a multinational pump and sprinkler company based in the LA suburbs. The timing seemed perfect: my mother, who had given up a promising career as an aerodynamics engineer (perhaps more promising even than his), had tired of always being left behind with two young children; one Saturday afternoon, she gathered the family, made a quiet and cursory announcement, and walked out for good. Bewildered and grieving, he scooped us up, me and my brother, and immigrated. Southern California in the late '70s was a magically artificial land of quietly ticking sprinklers presiding over rich green lawns, where being a divorcé and a single father was an opportunity, rather than the shameful secret it had been in our village. All the other white kids' parents were divorced.

During a school break one late spring, he took me along on a driving tour of large-scale irrigation in the Central Valley, just the two of us. It must have been when I was fourteen; I know this because when I was thirteen we all had to go back to England suddenly, in the middle of the spring school term, for an appointment at the US Embassy in Grosvenor Square to legalize our tenuous visa status and get our 'green cards'. And by the time I was fifteen, he was soppily in love with the blonde Christian lady who would become my stepmother – and I was giddy with relief at having successfully orchestrated the handover to someone who could take care of him when I went off to university.

But at fourteen, I hadn't started catching the scent of adult independence on the wind, and my father was still my world. My older brother was almost college-bound that spring, and he was off for a week on the Colorado River with friends. It saddens me now, to remember how indifferent both my father and I, in our sealed dyad, were to my brother and his comings and goings. As I began to develop a precocious feminism, all I could see was an unusually emancipated father, committed to nurturing an unconventional daughter who would feel empowered to do anything; I failed for many years to see his sexist expectation, at the same time, that his son would simply buckle down and take care of himself. And thus I settled greedily into the prospect of extended time for just us.

Dad visited his major clients, farmers growing mega-orchards of almonds and cherries, multi-thousand acre plantations of corn or broccoli or tomatoes, fields of strawberries or lettuce or carrots that stretched until they dissolved in the smog. In Bakersfield, we stopped to eat at an old-fashioned place on a freeway frontage street that featured an unexpected row of Basque restaurants, and I had escargot for the first time. I felt brave and cosmopolitan, a worthy grown-up companion for a man who'd learned to cook while on postgraduate studies in Brussels. The snails tasted only of garlic and salt, butter, and basil; their rubbery texture seemed vaguely marine, until my teeth met on the sandy grit of the dry Valley.

Wherever we went in the next days, the fields were peppered with the bent backs of imported workers, whose labor my father was in part enabling – and vice-versa. But in the passenger seat of the dusty, air-conditioned Datsun, I let my thoughts recoil from the divergence between their migrant experience and mine. We drove for miles alongside the concrete channel of the California Aqueduct, the crucial artery of the State's heart, sunk amid the fields and invisible for most of its length. My father talked about the billions of dollars the State had invested in securing water distribution, but gradually he grew distracted and distant. Somewhere northwest of Fresno, he finally pulled over and rolled down his window to gesticulate at the flat field beside us, shimmering oddly in the white sunlight. 'Rice,' he said. 'They're growing rice in California. Rice paddies in a desert. All of this is madness. All of it.' He turned to me. 'Let's go home.'

The last invention credited to my father, ten years later, wasn't a grit-resistant pump or a low-flow, high-pressure sprinkler head. It was a portable, reinforced cardboard house. The team of engineers, community educators, and other workers traveling from village to village in remote areas of Ghana to dig wells and install community-owned pumps needed somewhere to live while they completed their projects; it had to be low-cost, easy to assemble and disassemble, and lightweight to transport. Hence, the cardboard house. This was Dad's last work – this, and the small orchard in a foggy valley in Oregon that he had fallen in love with and where he hoped one day to retire. For a time, he spent half of each year in Ghana (with occasional side trips elsewhere: Senegal, Ethiopia, Haiti, Albania). He worked with rural community leaders – listening to their concerns around water availability, sanitation, disease, and provision for livestock; together, they would determine how to align with their needs a well, a pump, and training to support its ongoing maintenance by the community. And he could still be home at the orchard from springtime through the peach and pear harvests. My stepmother, who spoke reasonable Spanish, translated for the resident foreman who supervised the seasonal-migrant fruit pickers, while my father worked to gain proficiency in the language. When Dad was killed there one day, working alone on heavy machinery although he should have known better, the foreman thought my hysterical stepmother was making an error in translation and at first refused to believe it.

*

'Nothing is written,' says T. E. Lawrence with all the conviction of the dreamer-zealot to the skeptical warrior, Sherif Ali, played with homoerotic smoulder by the gorgeous Omar Sharif. Ali stares back at him from the bottomless wells of his beautiful sad eyes, just as he will stare silently some three movie-screen hours later when his beloved Lawrence – broken and disillusioned – walks away forever from Arabia and the fight for independence, back to his fat country of Oxfordshire.

I've never been to Ghana, but I've read that in a remote village in the Kwahu Afram Plains South district, about five hours' drive from the capital, Accra, a well was named in my father's honour. The extensive provision of wells in the region in the late 1980s, to replace the use of muddy and distant waterholes, resulted in the eradication of water-borne Guinea worm disease and the horrific suffering that accompanied it. About 60 per cent of those wells have since run dry; perhaps my father's is one of them. But there is reason to hope, at least, that the Guinea worm will never return.

*

My husband, who never met him, wonders aloud: might my dad have been passing intelligence to the British government? So many strange international assignments, and an odd portfolio of skills for a quiet northerner whose father ran a plumbing supply business. After all, plenty of people had clandestine connections in those days. I did venture to ask my mother once, as in the last decade or so it's begun to feel fairly safe to mention my father to her. She swore she would have known if it were so – my Cambridge-educated mother, who herself might have looked like a good candidate to either of the two Cold War networks that once recruited so successfully there – and she didn't. But it doesn't matter really whether he was or not – to me, at least. Either way, his life curved in strange parallel with the Anglo–American late-twentieth century, tracing its tracks of privilege and ideology, its evangelical confidence and waste, and also its slow-dawning awareness – perhaps not entirely separate from those other phenomena – that water and land (and, I like to think, *listening, local knowledge,* and *mutual cooperation*) are more crucial and potent determinants of global survival than any nuclear warhead.

And whatever the truth, for me there are more than enough mysteries and unanswered questions about him, about him and me, and about what it means now to have been his daughter. What it means to remember him asking, what should I do to make the world better?

*

There are ghostly layers of languages out at the edge of the bay, as well as the palimpsest of changing land uses. The wildlife refuge and the sewage plant are both named Las Gallinas, after the chicken ranch that was here in the 1800s on land granted from the nearby Spanish Mission. The Coast Miwok people called the nearby settlement Awani-wi, *red ochre baskets*; early white chroniclers recorded the names of nearby villages as Shotomko-cha and Nanaguani, but their accuracy is uncertain. The nuclear missiles were Nikes, after the Greek goddess of victory from whom my own given name somehow derives, via a crooked path through European variants of St Nicholas and a whimsical fashion in British girls' names when I was born. The manufacturer's name on the center-pivot apparatus, there in its faded circle, is not that of the company that brought us to California (Rain Bird: a name from Native American myth), but of one of its competitors. And then there are all the names of the plants and birds, native and migratory, that I have yet to learn, although I try to identify more all the time and add them to my phone notes until I have them memorized. Each has multiple names I need to learn or find, in Latin, English, Spanish, and Miwok.

I do know the northern harrier, *Circus hudsonius*. It hovers low over the abandoned shoreline fields – this one a female, dappled brown, with lemon-yellow talons and the keen face of an owl. She carries the name, rendered in Latin, of yet another English explorer-colonizer. She is hunting. Harrier was also the name borrowed for one of the military aircraft my parents both helped design, before I was born. I would have liked simply to point out that connection to my father, perhaps while walking with him along the raised dike separating the salt flats and the faded fields. That path will soon be part of a connected Bay Trail, enabling walkers to encircle the whole great bay, from San Francisco to Napa and all the way back around – unless the rising water gets there first.

With thanks to Mayo Thompson for permission to play on the title of the Red Krayola's 1967 album, *The Parable of Arable Land*.

THE SHORTLISTED ESSAYS

JENNY CHAMARETTE

Q IS FOR GARDEN

(ON SISSINGHURST, LEMON VERBENA AND SNAILS, PASSING, HERITAGE AND BOTHNESS)

Between the scarlet branches of the dogwood and the lilac-flowering hibiscus in my South London garden, there is an undersized lemon verbena plant. It is in the wrong place, overshadowed by the large arcs of the cherry tree that shed pink snowfall in May. Still, it shoots up tall stalks, fighting for light. I should move this little twiggy bush, which in its original location on Earth would become a tree of two metres or more. But there isn't much room in the borders of my urban garden, and I love the smell of its leaves as I brush past: a fresh, sweet, not-of-this-place scent that is nothing like the earthy mildness of the other vegetation around it.

A swatch of its pruned stems has lain drying on my kitchen counter top for days. As I pull papery leaves from twiggy cuttings, a small snail shell falls onto the pages of the book in front of me. Ten minutes later, a head and two stalked eyes emerge from a thin, grey-blue body, sliding silently across the page.

Q IS FOR GARDEN

This tiny hermaphrodite entered my kitchen, hidden in the leaves of a medicinal plant once thieved from South America by eighteenth-century European Spanish botanists. I love to say it this way, *thieved*, just as Jamaica Kincaid does in her book, *My Garden*. As Kincaid beautifully expresses it, gardening is often a result of botanical theft. In Spain, the lemon verbena became *Hierba luisa*. It travelled to Paris, Oxford, London, then throughout Britain, where it became a plant of many names: *Aloysia citrodora, Aloysia triphylla, Lippia citrodora*.[1] Finally it was shipped to North America, completing the cycle of larceny by landing in the epicentre of capitalism.

Those curling leaflets shelter an intersex being. Plants, by the way, are also mostly hermaphroditic, intermingling more-than-male and more-than-female parts. An intersex snail-being and a polysexual plant-being sit on my countertop, while I stand next to them, a human being caught up in the binaries of human sex and gender wars.

*

It feels obvious to say that the land is many-gendered. Sexuality is part of the contract between humans and the earth, which we either choose to cultivate or ignore. But to say that it feels obvious, does not mean that it is. To say there is a Q in garden, does not mean that you can see it.

You could say that this is a story about snail sex. It's about other things too: what you see and what you want to see, straight lines and queer spirals, passing and tenderness. Cultivation and civilisation, nature and ornament. Both, and. But it begins with a plant, and a snail.

*

On a mild late October morning, dry and a brief reprieve from the month's torrents hurled from the sky, a prominent journalist complains about queerness. I say prominent, but I had not heard of him before his column erupted onto my Twitter timeline. He lambasts the attempts of British heritage charity the National Trust to put queerness back into the history of Knole House in Kent. He describes the organisation's attention to the sexual histories of stately homes and their owners as an 'act of modern narcissism' that 'pull[s] the rug out from under our own feet.'[2] Strong words, uttered with conviction.

But as soon as you begin to deconstruct it, the thinness of the argument makes it feel like punching wet toilet paper.[3] Why Knole's queer history should be destabilising or amoral is left to the reader's imagination. The journalist's language speaks volumes, though, and is powerful enough to chime with other, more powerful individuals. The 'Common Sense' group of Conservative MPs recently condemned the National Trust for publishing a report on the historical connections of the stately homes in its portfolio to slavery and colonialism. Queerness is, apparently, like slavery in that regard: a threat to history, or at least 'a history that gives [...] a sense of roots.' Those lovely, white, straight-down-the-middle roots, which the columnist calls the origins of Britishness.

Back in my kitchen, I pull leaves from a plant pilfered by 250 years of colonial botany. The snail, eye stalks protruding, looks up at me. I look down at them, and I say,

'What the fuck is he talking about?'

*

Knole is a place familiar to my childhood in the suburban hinterland between Greater London and Kent. I studied Knole for my History GCSE. But that was in the time of Section 28, the legal framework set up by Margaret Thatcher's government that criminalised the 'promotion' of homosexuality by local authorities, ergo prohibiting any mention of it at all. Queerness in my history lessons was outlawed. Still, Knole is the birthplace of Vita Sackville-West, and former home of Edward Sackville-West, Vita's cousin. Both were queer, and part of the loose association known as the Bloomsbury Group.

Eddy Sackville-West, novelist and music critic, bequeathed a substantial art collection to his former lover Eardley Knollys, who in turn bestowed it to Mattei Radev, the former lover of E. M. Forster. The Radev Collection was exhibited in the early and mid 2010s in museums and galleries throughout the UK, and contains works by Picasso, Braque and Modigliani, as well as work from Bloomsbury artist Duncan Grant. And, just for luck, a black-and-white cat with an enormous bowl of cream in poster paint by six-year-old Pat Berrisford, displayed in 1953 at the national exhibition of children's art during the Festival of Britain.[4]

Vita Sackville-West, the writer and gardener, whose open marriage to Harold Nicolson enabled her to build Sissinghurst gardens, was famously a lover and friend of Virginia Woolf, who, inspired by Vita, so it is said, wrote *Orlando*. The journalist, he of tissue-thin argument, doesn't mention Vita by the way, only Eddy. Perhaps it's too much to include a woman in his diatribe about the uprooting of Britishness. An openly bisexual woman at that, who discussed her gender ambivalence in letters to her friend; who might have identified as non-binary, had the terminology existed at that time. The notion of a third, intermediate gender was prevalent in the Europe of Woolf and Sackville-West, particularly in Weimar Germany. Virginia certainly thought that Vita lived between genders.

Q IS FOR GARDEN

I am not sure what is so uprooting about an art collection, a garden and a great work of literature. If we know more about the sexual relationships that brought these art forms into existence, wreathed by friendship, creativity, and inspiration, then I can't see where the narcissism lies. But then again, I don't expect a paper-thin columnist to be able to explain himself. I can do the digging.

The Bloomsbury circles of lovers, artists, writers, gardeners, landowners and bequeathers unravel all the conventional mappings of heterosexual heritage. Their geometries break down the lines of father-to-son ownership, where each male proprietor produces male offspring-owners through assorted wives and lover-vessels. But in Vita and Eddy, the vertical columns of patrilineal heritage are displaced by squares, circles, triangles. Whorls and spirals.

This is what the journalist wants to straighten out, the queer Bloomsbury kinks and twirls. He wants to strafe the historical landscape, so that everything is pleasantly, heterosexually aligned. And mask queerness in the mystifying forces of inference, which is where the 'fun' is, apparently. If 'the fun is in the inference', then ignorance must be equally enjoyable.

All the queers must be closeted again so they don't disturb the jolly straight lines.

The journalist takes issue with the naming of queerness as a historical precedent. If 'queer' is just a name or an anachronism, not an act, or a life, or a being, then it can't have existed in the past. To use the word about earlier generations of landowners is abhorrent to the journalist, because 'they did not think like us'. They, is for them in the past, the ones from whom we are completely removed. Less than a hundred years ago, and we can't know them. What name could adequately describe lesbian and gay and bisexual relationships, the polyamorous dynamics of the gay salon, the mutual love and admiration between Vita and Virginia, and the gender ambivalence which inspired Virginia to write one of the most well-known works of modernist literature? Maybe all these things should have no name at all, so that they can be swept like dust into the back of that cosy, inferential closet.

In this journalist's straitened world, there are no – for want of a better word – queer spirals dancing between past and present. Any hint of queerness, anachronistic or not, must be obscured, ignored, at best inferred. Queers are narcissistic and uprooting. Queers are uncomfortable. There is no need to recognise queerness, only misrecognise it. On their trip to Knole, the journalist and his male companion are misrecognised as gay from their matching Barbour jackets; he is enraged. Because misrecognition should only happen to other people. Should only happen to queer people.

Tissue thin, and infinitely revealing.

The truth is that codicils of non-heterosexual love and aristocratic wealth did propagate the Bloomsbury circles of art and land, gardens and literature. These wellsprings of desire not only manifested themselves in which lover to take, but how to embody love in writing; how to pass works of art that stemmed from love from one lover to another; how to build the deep, rhythmic love that cultivates gardens from land.

The journalist who doesn't want to know about Eddy Sackville-West's lovers calls himself a historian. I do not know the name for a historian who wishes to eradicate the history that he finds dull or inconvenient. I did not know it was the work of a historian to erase history. Or love, for that matter.

There is something else, though. A needling. I can hear it. I can feel it.

The journalist's unreasoned reasoning for the strafing of history is a casual dismissal. Who one's lover is, isn't interesting, or important. Not real history. Who one's lover isn't, is of course very important indeed (Barbour jackets and all). For this journalist-historian, identity politics (under which category gay salons, *Orlando* and Sissinghurst all apparently fall) are dull, reductive. Lovers are ephemeral; not the stuff of history. Love is ephemeral too; nothing to do with heritage. And sexuality of course, is merely who you sleep with.

Ah. There it is.
I have heard this one before.

*

The hot-water infusion made from lemon verbena is anti-pyretic, anti-spasmodic, and said to relieve symptoms of PMS. For this reason, verbena is associated with the feminine. No reason why soothing tinctures should be the reserve of beings who menstruate, though.

The snail creeps along the thin edge of the kitchen paper I have set down to gather the dried verbena leaves. Their shell is glass-like, reddish brown. Even though they are less than a centimetre in diameter, the whorl of their shell is clear and distinct.

Land snails have complex reproductive sexualities. They may mate with another snail using their penis, or they may allow themselves to be penetrated by the penis of said other snail, or both at the same time. Some may, instead, self-inseminate. It doesn't really make sense to decide upon the binary gender of a snail, since they contain at least, if not more than, two.

Snail sexualities and mating practices are slow, led by touch, taste and smell. When a snail picks up on the chemical traces of a potential lover, it takes some time to reach them. Once they do, and after many hours of embracing, they shoot a love dart into their snail-lover to test out their partner's sexual probity. A sharp structure made of chitin and calcium, a love-dart's puncture would be the human equivalent of being stabbed by a 15-inch knife.[5] Snail sex is a risky transaction. They don't make snap decisions about sexual partners.

If I were to talk to the snail about sex, they would no doubt be cautious. Sex and sexuality are a sensuous, dangerous, whole body-mind exercise. Besides, a snail is more likely to identify the traces of my pheromones or feel the air vibrations of my voice, than hear me. Hearing is not a virtue in the world of gastropods.

'Sexuality is who you sleep with?'

The snail waggles their eye stalks.

*

I have heard this claim before.

Some years ago, on the last fine, warm weekend of the year before the long descent into deep autumn and moonlit afternoons, a friend and I took a long walk. This old friend and I, we talked deeply as we passed through the same Essex farmland and riversides that John Constable once painted.

I find myself re-walking this path, reliving the part of the conversation that caught me in a tender place.

Passing a churchyard, and for reasons that are beyond me, I tell my friend about the recoil I have felt in the past, like a hand closing around my throat, during the weddings of straight friends. Not because of the weddings, or the friends who wed, but because of the tightening of a bind that that leaves no room for my own queerness. The bind that feels like a metal hasp around a black tarpaulin that stifles weeds and wildlife. I don't explain myself very well, because the friend doesn't see the bind or the tarpaulin. Instead, he says: 'but why should it matter who you sleep with?'

As I press lemon verbena leaves into a jar, the snail curves their smelling lobes towards me. They wrap around the corner of the kitchen paper and retract swiftly, returning to the fragile safety of their glassy shell.

'But why did you tell him that?'
   The snail is motionless, muffled by the home on their back.

Q IS FOR GARDEN

*

Sissinghurst Castle, Vita Sackville-West's former home, is now a pleasure garden for most of the year. A place for lovers of plants, lovers of lovers, and lovers themselves, to seek pleasure in being with what grows there. Although I have visited many times in summer, with queer and straight friends, in autumn it is easier to see the garden's bones. Ligaments and nerve bundles too: small black signs pushed into the earth with white capitals that list the Latin binomial titles for what grows above or is hidden beneath the soil. In late November, it is easier to see the fresh planting among the perennials, some cut back, others with straggling limbs that will protect them from the frosts to come. Even on the cusp of winter, the rose garden gives off rose scent.

When Vita Sackville-West first started writing about her gardens, she was not an expert gardener. Her first garden experience was love, not mastery. The end stanza of her 1915 poem, 'The Garden' is about failure: 'We waited then for them to grow/ We planted wallflowers in a row/And lavender and borage blue/But love was all that ever grew.' Where lavender and borage struggle by implication ('But love'), love is what grows in Sackville-West's first garden in Long Barn, two miles away from her childhood home of Knole, and fifteen years before she and Harold move to Sissinghurst.

Vita's career as a garden designer did not begin with Sissinghurst; nor did her life as a writer end with it. On Sissinghurst's twenty-year development in *House and Garden* in 1950, she complains about the absence of straight lines in the old Tudor walls. They are 'coffin-shaped', 'oblique', 'inexplicable'. It takes queer Vita and her queer husband, Harold, to bring the lines into parallel, beginning the formal structure of the garden rooms, which she observes from her study in its all-seeing turret.

I find myself looking for straight lines in this bare-boned autumnal garden, but what I see are geometries, bends and returns. I see the coffin-shaped courtyard, but also the imperfect squares of the White Garden, which at this time of year is green. Delicate frothing grey-greens of Artemisia and Angelica, stout bottle-and-lime greens of box hedging, wavering yellow-greens of wisteria peeling away from its branches, filled with the steep sweaty scent of fallen apples. The Tudor walls are stacked with lichens and mosses; sturdy supports for the roses, clematis and old magnolias that lean between them and the Tower that houses Vita's writing room and her collections of blue Tehran glass. All the garden's geometries point towards spirals, circles, helical forms. Queerness in the straight.

*

The snail's long slim body slides along the underside of the discarded branches on my kitchen counter top.

'What possessed you to talk about passing?'

Passing is a tactic of safety performed by marginalised people who can appear, for a while, to be straight, or white, or cis-gendered, or able-bodied, or Anglo-European, or middle class. If performed for too long or too hard, passing overloads a body, becoming unsafe, self-estranging. Passing is always unstable, at risk of provoking hostile reactions from either of the identity groups the passer passes between (straight/gay, white/black, cis/trans, abled/disabled).

In Nella Larsen's 1929 novel *Passing* – now a film directed by Rebecca Hall and released at the Sundance Film Festival in 2021 – middle-class Irene simultaneously adores and defends herself against narcissistic, worldly and white-passing Clare. Two African-American women who pass as white, permanently or temporarily, battle with their confusing mutual attraction, amid the painful complexity of class, race and sexuality in 1920s Harlem. Passing is about class, race, sexuality, gender. It is also part of a much longer discourse from the histories of slavery. It is a matter of repressive violence and social control. Passing reaches into any domain where social dominance is regulated by who is included and who is excluded, by virtue of their appearance. It is – can be – a source of pleasure and danger, pride and shame. The experiences that flow beneath passing are historically powerful, life-altering. Yet passing is delicate: it provokes pain and incites tenderness. Its instability is just as likely to wound as it is to resolve.

Why did I bother trying to explain, on that perfect autumn day, the psychological toll of passing? Was it the churchyard and its associations with weddings past? Was it a rare moment of desire to reach out to someone not like me, to affirm the queerness in which I stand, in the land through which I walk? Was it because I felt safe? Or unsafe?

Clearly I must pass very well at times, or very badly, depending on how you see it. Because there is a sudden turn in the conversation, a fork in the road that jars and disorients me. An attempt, deliberate or unconscious, to reject the existence of passing. To discard the bind which I feel and he doesn't, my friend turns abruptly to my concern with plants and earth, my love of gardens and allotments, and what I have shared with him about the trees or wildflowers we walk past. With bold confidence, he names these things as part of a heterosexual, bourgeois world. Names them as definitively straight. A conclusive proof of my non-queerness.

I don't know why knowing about plants is supposed to be heterosexual, but I can make an educated guess.

The Swedish botanist Carolus Linnaeus first created classifications for flowering plants in the Latin binomial system, using binary models of sexual difference (male/female) to catalogue plants which themselves contain sexualities and genders infinitely more complex than a binary sexual system could ever accommodate. In the Linnaean binomial system, gender and sexuality are almost always either/or. And according to my friend's either/or system, knowing about plants is bourgeois and heterosexual and therefore nothing else.

According to these sorting systems, there is no space for the things in between. No room to love the mingling of the organic and the ornamental. The messiness of queer love in nature and cultivation is as unviable as a queer desire to speak about how plants came to be in an Essex riverside, or churchyard, or cottage garden. Nothing queer, then, about trying to decipher their ecologies, the long-fingered outcomes of European empires that imported innumerable plant species for decorative or utilitarian or even accidental reasons, regardless of their position in the ecosystem, or their capacity to accommodate, dominate, even eradicate other more fragile beings.

Because botany and ecology and gardening are often associated – and for good reason – with wealthy white heterosexuality, with land ownership, with patrilineal heritage, with colonial models of scientific classification, in the Linnaean binomial system, and in my friend's system, they cannot also be queer. There is no Q in garden or gardening or landscape or horticulture or cultivation because this is an either/or situation. No space for both, and.

*

By talking about passing, was I trying to destabilise the roots of a heterosexual monoculture? Or was I seeking to cultivate a tender, queer plant in inhospitable ground?

Either/or? Both/and?

The snail's newly-emerged antennae undulate in cosine curves.

'What the fuck are you talking about, now?'

Let me try to explain.

*

Queerness does not run straight, even as it seeks to even out centuries of obliquity. Queerness is not an either/or equation.

I doubt the journalist who dislikes the queerness of Knole would like Sissinghurst very much – it has been cared for by the National Trust since 1967.

Q IS FOR GARDEN

There is little inference in the Sissinghurst that Vita writes about from 1950, only clarity about struggle, time and waiting, and the energy to persist. She is clear about the physical-architectural lines drawn by her husband. How his imaginal world on paper devised the rooms and vistas of the garden, before they were created in earth and brick, stone and yew hedging. Vita's deference and love for her companion of decades shine out from the page.

And I see straight lines of a sort in the garden rooms of Sissinghurst. I also see mazes, turnings, oblique angles, the curve of the yew hedge, the tenderness of decay and senescence, and quiet new growth. I see circular time: the failing of plants from disease or the wrong positioning, or simply the end of their life cycle. Before-time, in the re-shaping of the old rose garden into the White Garden, which took place during Vita's lifetime. And after-time in Delos, the Greek island-inspired corner that Vita and Harold never managed to establish successfully. It is difficult to make Mediterranean planting thrive in rich, wet Kentish Weald. But by transforming the soil structure beneath, contemporary garden designer Dan Pearson and Sissinghurst's gardeners have created a future-time for Delos, with gravel and flagstone paths that snake between sandstone follies, structural euphorbia and grasses, scented thyme and achillea.

Why should straight lines always be perfectly and only straight? Couldn't they be lines of sight, pulled off-centre by the green flesh of plants, a tangle of branches, a winding path?

Vita writes consistently about her love of Sissinghurst. Love is a prerequisite for gardening: 'One needs years of patience to make a garden; one needs deeply to love it, in order to endure that patience. One needs optimism and foresight. One has to wait.'[6] Years of getting it wrong and starting again. Years of hope, despite living through two global wars. Years of waiting. Years of becoming used to failure as well as success. Years of labour (not all Vita's, as she admits herself).

Time undoes straight lines. Or maybe they were never straight to begin with.

Is Vita Sackville-West un-queered by her love of plants? Or is her garden rightfully a part of the queer heritage of gardening that runs back through the nineteenth century via the likes of Gertrude Jekyll, Maria Theresa Villiers aka Mrs C. W. Earle, and the Kewriosities – women trained as gardeners at Kew Gardens, who became sensational not because of their plant skills, but because of their bloomers?

Q IS FOR GARDEN

What if the queerness in gardening was a both/and situation?

The Kewriosities are another story. Q is for curious, for women's rights activist, for plantswoman.

*

Both, and.

Sexuality is both who you sleep with, and how you see the world. How you love it. Straight lines, obliques, coffin-shapes. Spirals, circles, helixes. Roses and sandstone. A plant and a snail.

And passing is painful. Misrecognition hurts. The difficulty of passing (or failing to pass) and the pain of misrecognition are common experiences for many queer people. And it's funny how, the more fragile and precarious your sense of being recognised is, the more you recognise yourself. What forms an identity most powerfully is what tries to extinguish it.

And patrilineal straightness unwittingly leaves its monocultural abrasions on land and bodies, past and present. But things regrow from whatever is broken, or needled, or wounded. Bodies and land learn very quickly how to self-tend, uproot the damage and reseed, regrow. The fungal fingers that notice the uprooting, they self-tend too, mending the broken links that stretch tenderly beneath the soil for leagues in a vast mycorrhizal network. And what comes up as queer might well have bloomed as something else at another time. *Hierba luisa*. Aloysia citrodora. Lemon verbena. These plants are connected even if the words are not.

And there is a history decided by a journalist who doesn't like what he sees because it disturbs the confident foundations of his straight, white, male world. There is also a probing history that looks for the gaps, revealing the erasures, planting wildflower meadows in churned-up terrain. Nobody ever said history was comfortable. Probing, spiral histories are destabilising for those more used to being the strafers than the strafed, the needlers than the needled. Those who walk on the land as if land were a birthright, and not a gift.

A plant and a snail could teach a different story. About a world, and a natural history, that is neither comfortable nor singular. Neither male nor female. Straight nor gay. Is more both/and. And until a new word comes along: queer.

And queerness is not so much about the naming as the feeling. Feelings. Both the feelings – my feelings – of being needled constantly, in an endless bind to an inhospitable world, and the love, the tenderness, finding a space to grow between. A fragile helix the thickness of a snail shell, from which to emerge and retreat. To come out and go in again.

There is no need for a Q in garden, if you do not see the Q. And there is no stronger need for that Q, than when it can't be seen.

'I see you.'

The snail slowly meanders across the countertop, seeking shelter.

I see the snail, too. Their many-gendered, polymorphous fragility. Shell and flesh. Eye stalks and lovedarts.

Both, and.

Vita Sackville-West's gardens run through her. As do her disinheritance and extraction from Knole, her childhood home; as do her wealth and status that made manual labour a thing that others do, except in times of global crisis. World War II left her with no more than blistered hands from trimming yew hedges: the same hedges which now observe perfect right-angles and geometric curves. These things co-exist with her queerness. They are uneasy. They are part of the oblique, enfolded outlooks that make a life a life, and not a straightened historical certitude.

Like many people with a pot of soil or two, a handful of seeds, gardening is part of my being. It is generative and gutsy: plunging my hands into the earth is one of the most intimate acts I can imagine. That intimacy is no more governed by who I sleep with than the golden, sun-ripened sweetness of an allotment-grown tomato.

And yet.

Sexuality is not a thin cultural veneer, but grows deeply from creativity and life force. It runs deeper than history: it is the earth from which history grows. The land is many-gendered. They say that 'civilization' is four days deep, but cultivation goes far deeper. All these things are in unique partnership at any given time. They are not, and never have been determined by the cultural misconceptions of a so-called historian. No matter how powerful the system of naming.

The seeds of my being have learned to flourish and transform under tricky environments. When I pull a weed, or plant a seed, I am not always, maybe even rarely successful in cultivating my spirit, entwined as it is with plant and animal life, lemon verbena and land snail. If my tender shoots are unwittingly crushed by the misperceptions of a friend, who himself involuntarily emulates the binary language systems of eighteenth-century botanists, or the words of a twenty-first-century journalist, that story is as personal as it is political, cultural and historical.

Both/and.

*

By the time I have screwed the lid tight on the jar of verbena leaves, labelled it and put it away on the shelf, the snail has crawled off the kitchen worktop, looking for a safe place to hibernate. I hope they find it.

I write in the spirit of defiance and gentleness. Gentleness and defiance to tend my tender plants, in my tender landscape. The tender queer garden of my life.

And I also know this from a space of deep knowing-ness, where words and names are secondary to the evolution of being. I know this in the nape of my neck and the curve of my big toe as it presses into the earth beneath me. There is, always has been ample room for queerness in the matrix of tiny microorganisms and minerals, water acidities and leaf-mould, compost and humus.

In civilisation and cultivation; nature and ornament. Both, and.

LAURA COLEMAN

THE FENCE

JANUARY

Aidan is tall, with pale freckles across his nose. He's rarely seen without a Kronenbourg can in his large, scarred hand, a 'blue', if you want to buy one in the shop. He drives a silver van and he's a McAllister, part of one of the sprawling, entangled families that make up almost half this island's 106 population. It is not unusual to find yourself down the pier with a blue in hand, suddenly discovering yourself to be drinking not only with Aidan, but his mum and dad, his brother, a sister, an uncle, a few of his cousins and – often – a ninety-year-old granny too.

We stand as usual in 'the waiting room', huddled in the cold-tiled chamber, the smoky, whiskey-drenched rain-safe space between the key compass points of island business. The bar, the shop and post office, the outdated beige museum, the toilets. There are people who spend their lives in here, waiting as the name suggests. Their uniform is yellow gumboots and sheep-and-diesel stinking oilskins, scaly woollen jumpers and knitted hats, skin leathery and crumpled from wind and whiskey. There is a low constant banter, heavy with tractors and boats, fuel and weather. Eyes watch the ocean whip across the pier, Hebridean waves melting turquoise, green and grey. Snow on the mainland, a sheet of white making its way over the sea. Gannets and gulls dive for their lunches, as men and women roll their cigarettes, babies giggle, children play and collies lie out in the rain.

'So, this fence then,' I say. My voice is timid, and it sets me apart. Words in here are hurled crudely. I often find myself flinching. I straighten my shoulders, widen my stance and correct myself. 'This *fecking* fence!' My correction is met with approving glances, before a silence falls and expectant grins stretch over the rough faces, mostly Aidan's family, to see what he will do. Aidan holds the island monopoly on fencing. I have been trying to convince Aidan to build me a fence, for what feels like a long time. Three months, four? Since I moved here anyway. I want to keep the sheep and cows out of my garden, to set up an exploratory vegetable patch without it being trampled. I want my mother to visit with her dog without fear that the dog will massacre a sheep, and – mainland attitude or no – I want to know in my head what is mine. I ordered the fencing supplies a month ago, perhaps optimistically. The supplies have arrived, but Aidan is yet to appear.

Aidan takes a long sip of his blue. My eyes flicker outside to where my dog, Alfredo, is waiting anxiously on the road. His tail is down and island dogs circle him, feral collies mostly, sensing weakness. There is a pleading sort of panic in his gentle brown eyes, but I'm reluctant to step in. We both need to find a way to navigate here. I'm the only woman in the waiting room today, which is not unusual. I take a long swig from my own can, swallowing the cheap, cold beer. It is barely one in the afternoon and it is either a can or a whiskey dram for most people as we wait for 'the boat'. The boat's arrival from the mainland, with lifeline supplies, pallets of brown Amazon parcels, and – at this time of year – few visitors, can happen anywhere between four and zero times a week. It depends on the roughness of the westerlies, or – as the islanders claim – the whims of the captains. The boat, I have learnt, is this island's timeclock, along with the rising and setting of the sun, and the stock of blue, red and black cans in the shop.

Aidan stares thoughtfully out to sea, as if he has much to consider. Today the ocean is a two-tone band of slate on silver, the wind gusting at – according to my weather app – between 28 and 36 miles per hour. It is bitingly cold on my exposed cheeks, and I pull my scarf tighter. There is the scent of frost in the air. Even I know the boat will be touch and go today, the waves starting to slap the edges of the pier with vehemence. Aidan doesn't look at me, but the corners of his blue eyes crinkle slightly with a wry almost invisible laughter. He's wearing a woollen hat, which – indoors or out – I've never seen him without, and an ancient grey jumper under oilskins, probably as old as him. He pulls out a rumpled packet of tobacco and starts to roll.

'Aye,' he says.

It has taken him such a long time to speak that for a moment, I struggle to fathom whether he is talking to me. When I realise that he is, I look around, baffled. Aidan's father, Doug, grins from where he sits on a cheap plastic chair. He is king in the prime spot by the waiting room door. I am helpless. English. A mainlander. Doug takes another long swig of his golden whiskey. Jim, Aidan's cousin, stands just outside not minding the sudden pelting of heavy, freezing rain. He pulls the binoculars from his weathered face and chuckles, his bluff smile a white slash in the mist. I can't tell if he's amused by the lack of boat, or by my lack of fence.

I look back at Aidan again. 'Aye?'

'I'll do it this week, aye.'

I feel a rush of excitement. The sun bleeds out from behind one of the low-lying grimy clouds and casts a stripe of gold across the sea. I dance on the toes of my rubber boots.

'Really?'

Aidan shrugs, his eyes crinkling a little more. A rainbow appears, the colours sharp and opaque, before melting into the grey, halfway between here and the white-tipped mainland mountains.

APRIL

Piles of fencing materials lie in my line of sight. They have lain there long enough for the grass, sorrel and wildflowers to be growing up around them. As if they all believe the wooden posts and rolls of metal chain link to be as much a part of the scenery as the boulders that scatter the landscape, or the stream – 'burn' in Scots – that runs down the border of my garden. Wherever I am on the island, I can hear water. Today, a light spring day, there is the gentle rush of the burn, making its soft way down to the sea.

I'd bought my little bungalow, at the age of thirty-six, to leave England. I was going to live 'off grid', to hear the sea every day and take my partner, Alfredo, a socially anxious street dog from Lisbon, away from people, from shopping bags blowing in his face, from the sound of cars backfiring. I unzip my fleece and try not to grind my teeth at the sight of the half-buried fence posts. There is a cool breeze in the air and it smells of flowers, sand and seaweed. This is the first real sun we have had in weeks, and the touch on my skin feels wonderful, as if the world is just starting to wake up to the fact that winter is over.

THE FENCE

The sheep and their lambs know this already. They are busy, eating the roses that have just started to bud, colouring the front of my low white house pink. I've asked the sheep not to do this, but they don't retain instruction for longer than the time it takes for me to go back inside. It has become my habit to eat lunch looking out of my window, watching as they munch my garden to the quick. It is my daily soap opera, and it is morbidly fascinating. Hanna the farmer, tied to this island through partnership with another of Aidan's family, is kind enough to come and gather them up, if I let slip that her sheep have been decimating my roses. Their farm lies on the other side of the long black beach, and it isn't long before the sheep return, through whatever meandering pathways take them between the island fences. Their long black faces and spots of blue on their backs seem to change infinitesimally every time, as if they are new sheep come to torment me with their appetite for roses.

The sky overhead is the sort of soft spring blue that makes the world feel unusually gentle. A scattering of wispy clouds make slender kites over the hills that nestle the small valley in which my house is hidden. There are about twenty other houses on this side of the island. We are far from the pier and the beguiling draw of the waiting room, and the land is divided into crofts, old boundaries set out when the island was worked. Now, despite some resistance, crofts are starting to be parcelled out and sold off. I have three plots around me, about to go on the market. But at the moment, my house is still secret. I cannot see anyone from here, only the sea, the sheep, and the year-round occupants – the greylag geese. The burn gurgles merrily, connected to the spring from where I get my drinking water.

From where I sit, perched on one of the mossy rocks spread about, I see the ocean, flat metallic blue, about five hundred metres away across bracken-brown, nettle-rich fields, and the bay curves unhindered towards the Atlantic. If I turned around, I would see the imposing cliffs of basalt grey that, a long time ago, curved the edges of a glacier. These cliffs, ragged enough to catch clouds, will turn orangey pink as soon as the sun starts to drop. Everything is silent, all but the lazy dance of the water, the greedy baying of lambs, and the starlings and tits, the robins and skylarks also starting to wake up to spring. A golden eagle, one of four – two mating pairs – glides by on an updraft, on the hunt for food, perhaps for his nesting mate. This is the time for egg-laying. On skating white fluted wings, the bird soars back and up, disappearing into powdery clouds.

Aidan came by this morning.

THE FENCE

'Aye, next month maybe, aye.' A tendril of smoke from the coffee I'd made him had curled up into the feather-grey mist. The tall Finger of God, a black stone formation that stands atop the cliffs, pointed critically into the heavens. The Finger looks down on my house, as it presides over the fissure of rock that starts the waterfall, a cascade tumbling three hundred metres and more, into the valley of our little township. Today is a dry day, and the snake of water looks from here to be barely a trickle. Aidan still wore his oilskins though, despite the sun, sweat running down his forehead. Rain comes fast here, I have learnt, and no true islander seems to go far without a set of waterproofs in tow.

I'd gazed up at him, looming over the pile of fencing supplies. 'Aye?'

'Aye.' He'd sipped his coffee. 'I have to do Sam Connell's fence first, though.'

I'd blinked. This was the first I'd heard about Sam Connell. I tried to smile peaceably, but I wanted to punch his freckled pale nose, his ever-present oilskins, blue eyes and matching hat. I'd been waiting seven months! The old fence that had been left by the old owner, Clyde, seemed to lean closer every day, seemed to rot a little more, every day. It was half trampled by meandering cows. Useless. I wanted...I don't know what I wanted. To handle a simple manoeuvre? To have

66

an adult experience with the first house I had ever owned? To find someone, anyone in this place with a sense of urgency? But when I asked around… *Nae, just ask Aidan,* they'd said. *Aidan'll do it. Aidan does the fences here.*

'Aye.' He put down his cup, on the apex of the stack of fence posts. How long would it take before they started to rot? 'Sam's been waiting longer 'n you.'

'Longer than half a year?' I kept my voice calm. Calmish.

Aidan's eyes crinkled, as if he knew I wasn't calm at all. One of the greylag geese hooted, the sound reverberating off the cliffs, as they all spread their wings and set off into the breeze in pairs. The nights are shorter now and daffodils and wild strawberries are blooming in the verges. Aidan can no longer say: 'Ah, but it's winter, the weather's dreich!' Now he's saying: 'Aye but it'll be summer soon, there's too many tourists, I'm busy.'

I sit here with an unusual feeling inside me, as I look at the decimated roses, and the grass growing up through the fence posts. It is a tightness in my chest, despite the white tufts of fresh-born lambs, the bunnies sunbathing on the daisy-bright grass, the easy blue of the sky and the thickness and age of the moss coating this smooth rock.

THE FENCE

AUGUST

'See,' Hanna says with her soft, lilting Hebridean accent. 'It's not hard.'

I look between her and the fence post lying on the ground. The post, the 'strainer', she tells me it is called, is taller than me. It must be about my weight too. In contrast to the wee posts, the 'stobs', which I can lift relatively easily, these strainers are beasts. They should stand every twelve metres or so, to do most of the job of keeping the fence upright.

'Can I get by without them?' I ask hopefully.

'No.'

I gaze at the strainer. There are eighteen of them. Hanna shrugs, shielding her eyes against the sun as a buzzard swoops low over the grassy summer fields. Hanna taught herself to put up fences. The men told her she couldn't, but she did it anyway. It is untenable for her to be dependent on an oilskin-wearing 'teuchter'. Hanna thinks it is untenable for me, too.

If I listen carefully, I can just hear the wistful strains of the willow warblers, coming from the strand of bushy trees, in need of pruning, by the burn. In a few months, these warblers will be setting off on their long migration south, back to Africa. Although we are at the height of summer, and today I am wearing a t-shirt and shorts, I've already noticed that the days are getting shorter again. I track it, with the placing of where the sun sets. Every evening, it seems to move infinitesimally further south and soon it will no longer drop into the ocean, but behind the violet headland. I truly never thought time would move so fast here. But it does. There are no days of the week, no Mondays, Tuesdays or Wednesdays. Only boat days and non-boat days. In the distance, a white sheet of rain is advancing over the sea, navy blue today. Even from here, I can see the white tips riding across the surface of the waves and hear them, too, like a rushing breath. Where we stand in my garden, there is not a cloud in the electric sky. But that rain will reach us in minutes. Already, a full rainbow is gleaming north to south across the tangerine-stained cliffs, the pot of gold hidden somewhere deep in the purpling heather. It is not quite the season for rainbows, but it'll be here soon. September, October when the weather changes so fast, pulled in off the Atlantic and caught by the presiding cliffs, that the rain catches the sun countless times each day. That was when I moved here. September. A whole year has gone by.

I am uncertain whether I have enough reserves to handle eighteen of these strainers. I am uncertain whether I have enough reserves to handle even one of them.

'It takes me about half a day, to dig a hole for one of these nyaffs.' Hanna taps the butter-pale post with the toe of her leather boot. It doesn't move.

THE FENCE

'Without a tractor, you'll have to make the holes by hand. You'll need to get about half a metre deep.' She surveys me with a shadow of a smile. 'Expect lots of rocks down there.'

Oh, I want to say. I do.

The sea has become a blanket of haze. I can no longer see the horizon, and the hot air has suddenly turned thick, damp with the shock of drizzle. The first drops already dust my sweaty forehead, and it feels glorious. Hanna brushes a strand of wet fringe out of her hazel eyes. Her boots are solid on the earth, and her gaze moves over the land.

I watch as Bobby, Hanna's cheerful collie, and Alfredo play in the shelter of the shockingly pink rhododendron bush. Both are trying to hump the other, but it is good natured. Alfredo's long, brown face, usually on high alert and etched with shadows, is relaxed. He doesn't wear a collar, or a lead here. In the last few months, he hasn't been jumping at strange sounds so much. And sometimes – *sometimes* – when we are sitting up on the hill together, and the day is at its calmest, he will forget for a moment that he is always afraid, and he will meet my eyes. This is something he hasn't been able to do in the six years since we have been together.

Hanna and I sit shoulder to shoulder in the wet mud, sheltering in a small dip in the wall of the hill as the rain passes overhead. Aidan has a tractor.

Hanna tells me blandly that it would take Aidan all of a day to put in all eighteen of these strainers. I wish I had a tractor, I think, as she counts the sheep speckling the hillside. The grass is thick with yellow buttercups, purple orchids and the thin, miraculous bodies of magic mushrooms. Bobby and Alfredo continue to dance, heedless of the now cascading sheets of rain. For a moment, Alfredo considers showing Bobby the private nest he has been working on these last months, underneath the rhododendron, but he thinks better of it. They aren't that close, after all. Give it a few more months. The rainbow has disappeared. It is all rain now, only a faint glimmer of gold hinting at the sun that will soon reappear, just resting on the far side of these low-lying fat clouds. Turadh, Hanna tells me, is the name for a break in the weather between showers.

OCTOBER

The sheep have all gone. I haven't seen them around my garden for a while. I was down at the pier when a lot of them, hundreds by my count, were pressed into a trailer, the familiar blue marks on their bottoms forced hard against the metal sides, and off they went on the boat, to be sold at market somewhere far away. I miss them. My roses have grown exponentially, and show no sign of easing as the cold starts to draw in. The sweet smell of them fills my

THE FENCE

garden. Alfredo sits patiently on top of his rock, the gurgle of the burn at his back, carefully assessing my progress as I stack firewood against the side of the house. This wood arrives in 'a cube', one cubic metre in a hessian sack, delivered straight from the island forestry. Jim delivers it, in one of the island tractors, the red one rather than the grey, and it is polite to offer him a dram of whiskey in return. The wood today is wet, unseasoned, heavy with weight. In some of the logs, I can see the blush of mould starting to grow, staining the insides with strange kaleidoscopic patterns. This is the fifth cube I have had delivered this month, and I am hoping it will be enough to last me through the winter, if it dries in time. My house, like most here, has no electric heating. Our electric grid, functioning on renewable energy, cannot support it, and so we make do instead with open fires and wood burners, feeding through to a back boiler that heats the water, and the radiators. I have a small open fire, and my house is barely insulated. It got cold last winter. I was hoping to replace it for a wood burner by now, but workmen don't come out here from the mainland much and I wonder now how long it might take for me to figure out how to insulate my loft, to find someone to bring over a new wood burner. It'll happen at some point, I suppose. And I've gotten used to wearing a few extra clothes. Alfredo sleeps under the blanket anyway.

LAURA COLEMAN

DECEMBER

It is frosty. My cold fingers press into the grass, breaking ice-crests with satisfying sighs. A full moon shines overhead, painting the cliffs behind me startling colours. Our breath, Alfredo's and mine, blows out white, tufting through the darkness. Clyde, the aging, stubborn, gentle man who sold me this part of his croft, was one of the last people on this island to speak Gaelic as his first language. He grew up here. His ancestors were born here, in the black stone house that stood on this plot before it burnt down, thirty years ago, and they rebuilt with my nineties bungalow. They got married here, died here. I see the memories in what Clyde left behind. In elderly, broken things that are spread out around me now. The antique tractor, just up on the hill's curve, half buried by St John's Wort. The hundreds of old plastic feed bags that I have been working on pulling out of the burn. The bones of the old sheep, submerged in the bank. The countless rusted screws and screwdrivers, the nuts and bolts I have scraped out of the rich brown mud. The old fence, too close to the house. He put it there so he would have less of a garden to maintain, but the wilderness that has grown up since he left seems to ache a little more each month, asking for space. The shattered glass, the barbed wire coils, the bottles and jam jars and eroded cans. The barely standing digger perched atop the rocks, and the rusted plough.

THE FENCE

The world around me is still. I take my gloves out of my pocket and slowly put them on, my fingers losing feeling. The waterfall tumbles not too far away, and it sounds heavy with the day's rain. I listen to it, the only sound apart from my heart, and Alfredo's, pressed warm against my side. The hydro, that powers the grid along with solar and wind turbines, will have been singing today. It was a wet day, a wet week, and the peace of this sudden dry cold feels like a gift. I press my gloved hands into the grass again, not caring about the damp that seeps through the wool. The earth is hard. Frozen solid.

We'd walked along the beach tonight, lit ashen by the rising moon, and the world had looked Nordic in its ferocity. One of Alfredo's friends had joined us, a wild sea-grey dog who leaps over her fences, and trots down the beach. Alfredo waits for her every day now, at the turn in the road where she lives, his tail wagging ferociously. They run together across the alien expanse, leaving a sea of stark prints behind them, as the dunes shift under the sea salt tang. The sand was black, scaled with ribbons of silver. Seaweed and washed up sea plastic – toothbrushes and fishing rope, mermaids' tears, fractured jerry cans and bottle tops – made inextricable webs. Jellyfish shapes, speckled transparent, rested across the bay waiting to be washed away in the next high tide. As we'd returned home in the dark, the waves pelted aluminium pale.

The shadow of my house is stark as the moon hangs above it, and smoke from the chimney curls like an upward gust off the waterfall. The cliffs look like they are made of sapphire. Some black shapes pass overhead, bats perhaps, maybe an owl. I am just north of the house, in the little cluster of birch, oak and spruce, beneath the familiar dark rope of my washing line, where I've hung buoys that I've collected off the beach by their coloured fishing ropes, Christmas decorations jangling in the notes of blue moonlight. In my oilskins, I look upwards. I am wrapped up so warm, layers make sweat pool along my spine. The sky is sheet dark and speckled with stars that are strong enough to shine through the light. The moon so bright it leaves a golden imprint on the backs of my eyelids. I can see Mars, blush red, above the Finger of God. I rest my hand in Alfredo's fur. He feels cold, because he has just been rolling in the frost, but his belly and heart are warm. Together, we listen quietly to the waterfall, to the burn that has flooded its banks a few steps away, raging to meet the sea.

It is hard to get rid of anything, when you are surrounded by the sea. What washes up, stays. What you put here, remains whether you want it to or not. If you buy a sofa, that sofa will stay for the rest of eternity, or until it is buried, and the elements take it. Cars, old boats, threshing gear from centuries ago – rusted and immobile – are this land's statues. Eroded, down to the stark truth of their bones. They cannot go back to the mainland, it is expensive, and where will they go anyway, when they get there? Landfill. They may as well stay here and be a memory. At least people will look at them and know their shape. It is the same in the waiting room. There are ghosts there too, in the eyes of the people watching the boat come and go. In the eyes of the people who were born here, and in those who washed up and stayed. Centuries, buried as layers of fossils pressed into the aged basalt of these cliffs.

I understand now that it is hard to make space and attention for new things, when the island is already so full. There is a relaxing that needs to happen, that I didn't understand when I arrived, if you want to stay here. I feel it happening in my bones, sometimes, like a slow lazy softening, and I see it happening to Alfredo. I also see that it makes it hard to leave, afterwards, once it has begun. Your bones start to fill up, like those cliffs with their fossils, and you feel somehow bigger than you were, and heavier. Clyde had been trying to leave for years. He'd had this house on the market for almost a decade, before I came. He's on the mainland now, but he's still here too, inextricably. In the stories and pieces that he couldn't take with him, or couldn't help but leave behind. There are 106 people, but sometimes it feels like there are a thousand, and at the same time only one or two of us. I really thought

I would feel smaller, when I came here. But I realise how wrong I was. We are giants, surrounded by water. Maybe because, here, there is nowhere to go, and no place to hide our discarded pieces.

MAY

'So, you're a proper islander now, aye?'

I spin, leaning my head back and laughing. I've kicked off my shoes, and I'm breathless, my arm nearly wrenched from the socket, but there is no slowing down. The floor is sticky with spilled beer and our fairy-lit, jewelled hall is full of sweat, the stink of wood smoke, and the whip-fast notes of the fiddlers, carving out the jig atop the stage with no hint of stopping.

'I am?' I pant, as Aidan throws me around in another spin and we 'strip the willow' down the long lines of exhausted dancers. The night sky through the windows is starting to pale, and the gloaming light stains our faces pink. Soon, outside where the trees grows, a cuckoo will start to call. Aidan spins the people to the left, I spin the people to the right, meeting each turn in the middle, the momentum carrying us buoyantly down to the bottom, like corks bobbing in a river, before another pair sets off. We will carry on spinning and spinning, for half an hour and more, a tradition amongst this island's ceilidh bands to leave the dancers wrung out and wild before the party ends.

THE FENCE

Aidan grins. The sound of the fiddles fill every pore and I sway, the music singing joy. I never experienced anything like this before I came here. Huge two- or three-day long parties where you know every person, where the jigs and reels go all night long, and the fiddles sing beneath the stars. Where eight- and nine-year olds dance barefoot with eighty-year-olds, where adults fall asleep alongside children wrapped up in sleeping bags at the back, and everyone sits outside by the fire as the sun comes up.

I stamp out the beat with my feet and laugh.

'Are you ever going to tell me then, why you hate fencing so much?'

He laughs, stamping his own feet, and shakes his head. It isn't an answer, but then we're launching off for another dizzy set. This is fierce, this feeling. Maybe it's answer enough. Every note in this jig is a fight, a grounding down of boot heels. Against the onslaught of weakness, against what might bring down this laughter, these people, these families. This island fought, twenty years or so ago, for independence. Saorsa: freedom. Liberation from the laird, the landowner, the English. They fought before that, against the Vikings, against the English again, against the clan lords and the priests. Against the weather and the draft of the young people away to the cities, to the office jobs and the mainland luxuries. Life here is easy now, the old folk say. There's electric from the island grid, as long as the batteries hold out and the wind blows. There are no more diesel generators that tie women and the light in their homes to their husbands, because they do not have the upper arm strength to start the power on their own. There's fibre-optic internet. People like me can buy a house here, and beyond the frustration of not being able to dig a hole for a strainer post without pulling our backs, we can make our livings off of our laptops, rather than our land.

But people like Aidan, who were born here. He lives in his caravan and sits in the waiting room watching the boats come and go. The island is his. There aren't a lot of jobs, fencing is one of the few. Mostly all he needs is the money to buy a few blue cans. So he does the fencing, even though it is not what he wants to do. It gives him enough to keep him here, to drive his silver van, to trek around with his camera taking pictures of the beaches, and of the stars, and to dance till dawn at the ceilidhs. I don't blame him. He tried the mainland. He hated that much more than putting up a few fences.

JULY

The early morning is orange, and it smells of wind. I have learnt that I live next door to a broonie. Brownies, I would have called them in England. There are many uncanny islanders here. Kelpies, mysterious, violent water horses that steal young women and dwell up in the dark ice-frozen lochans. Selkies, the seal-women. A ghostly washerwoman, the bean-nighe, who lives in a stream and filches the souls of the bladdered, the drunks, on their way home from the pier. Broonies, though, are peaceable, I've been told by Felice, the island's historian. Felice dresses up as one every Halloween and hides up on the hill to wait for the children to come and ask for her stories. It is best to feed broonies, she has told me, just to be safe, so I have left out bread and milk. I hope the broonie found it, rather than the thriving rat population. I sit now on the broonie hill, as this brisk wind ricochets past, heavy with the scent of pine brush, diesel and burning plastic from someone's rubbish dump. The brown-gold water of the burn slides by. I finished clearing it out this month, finally fishing through the last of the ancient feed bags and the sheep and otter bones. Up to my thighs, cold as hoarfrost and wildly awake, balancing precariously on the edge of the tiny white foamed waterfall, I'd scythed away the last of the brambles and thorny tangles, freeing the netted water crowfoot and white stars of grass-of-Parnassus.

There are no midges this early. The red fires of fuchsia flame in the dawn light, alongside frothy meadowsweet, water purslane, iris, hogweed, and cascading orange blossoms of montbretia. The birds have set to on their singing. I can hear the willow warblers again, flittering about the treetops, heavy with summer growth. They've been back for a while from their sojourn south. The most daring of a pair of robins, with a white flash of lightning on the underside of her tail, perches precariously above the fuchsia and cocks her head at me. She doesn't seem to mind the wind. I smile. Hardy. I hear the crowing of a cockerel. Alfredo waits at my side for his walk, his velvet ears ruffling, angled towards the sea. If I look like I have forgotten him, he will turn and press me with his nose. A year ago, he would have waited forever, rather than have me notice him.

Far away, the island is saturated with tourists and unlike winter, when the waiting room and the comfort of the warm lull of bawdy laughter and the heat fire of a whiskey dram seemed to drag me in, I don't go there now. I have an island timeclock and this is my hibernation time, when the summer days draw long and there are suddenly people whose names I do not know. I find I look for my own space under the bold openness of the skies.

Sheep with blue marks on their bottoms feast on my roses. Cows meander over the black beach, chewing on the seaweed and sleeping the heat out of the quartz sand. They will come up here later and stir my nettle-thick grass with manure. But I feel relaxed, cosy, although nothing much seems to have changed.

THE FENCE

My garden is wilder, the St John's Wort covering the tractor is blossoming. The old shed's roof has caved in, the burn is cleaner. The broonie is hopefully well fed, the grass has become tufty and coarse, because I do not address it with the blades of a lawnmower. I have grown a little fatter, my skin a little more tanned. Aidan got a new hat. His van broke down, but it has now been fixed. Jim got a new tractor. Three new babies have been born, and two couples have got married. Alfredo, who used to walk on tiptoes, now walks proudly, with his head held high.

SEPTEMBER

When Aidan arrives, I stare at him from where I am standing, up on the broonie hill. His new hat no longer looks new, and the bright green colour has faded to grey. The sight of Aidan and his van parked next to the burn is so surprising, Alfredo barks.

'Morning,' Aidan says.

It is indeed morning, the sun has barely crested the cliffs. Aidan pulls what looks like tools out onto the grass, his waterproof jacket hanging over his front seat. He's just wearing a t-shirt, his arms freckled from the late summer sun. The clouds are a thousand different greys.

'What are you doing here?' I exclaim.

'Thought I'd do your fence.' His blue eyes crinkle. 'Aye?'

LAURA COLEMAN

OCTOBER

The trees are turning golden yellow, and their burnished edges look like crowns. The purple heather has browned and there are concerts of rainbows, every day. The slow meandering pace of life no longer surprises me, even whilst the days fly by like the skittering swoops of oystercatchers on the beach.

I look up and realise that the willow warblers have gone.

I have started digging a vegetable patch, covering it with two years' worth of compost and gnarled old seaweed collected by the armful off the beach. When my vegetable patch is ready, I will plant the seeds my mum has collected for me, for a spring crop. Spring onions, chicory and purslane. I don't know if they'll grow, there's not much protection from the wind and I need to start thinking about planting some new trees, for a windbreak. But it feels good to get something in the ground. The sheep peer through the new fence at my progress with disparaging looks. Their liquid eyes take in the healthy, growing roses. There is still one of the sheep who manages to find her way in. She is very small, and either very smart or very stupid, because she cannot find her way out again and Alfredo and I have lost hours trying to reunite her with her friends. We don't mind. It doesn't matter. And it doesn't matter that Aidan has not finished the fence, like Alfredo who cannot count but always leaves two biscuits in the bottom of his bowl at supper time. There is still some wire that needs tensioning. What is left of the old fencing could be taken away to where Aidan has said he will be able to dispose of it, or at least hide it, in the quarry buried behind his dad's farm. There is a latch that needs to be attached to the gate, and two holes that need patching. But these are not big things. These are things that I can do.

I have put out the housewarming gift that my mother made for me, a stately blue vase, built for the garden and the grass. It sits now just beneath the rock that Alfredo favours, and I am not afraid that a cow will trample it. I sit there now, wrapped up in a hooded jacket and scarf as a flat brown breeze twists the tendrils of my hair. A low mist lolls over the headland, and I smell fallen leaves and autumn bonfires. It will be Halloween soon, and I must remember to leave out some milk for the broonie. Rain hangs around the garden, sticking to the trees and the last of their leaves. I breathe it in, and it fills my lungs completely. The garden is fresh air and space. There is no old fence separating me from the twinkling waters of the burn, and the new fence is far away and forgettable, exactly as I hoped it would be, in the pale light of another dying day. A golden majestic sheen touches the flat blue of the waves and Alfredo watches it, his ears gently fluttering in the breeze.

BEN CRANE

LAST FLIGHT OF THE GOSHAWK?

In the pre-dawn darkness of early autumn, I wake to the tiny tooth-drill whine of mosquitoes combined with the soft sounds of my dogs Etta and Flash breathing on the bed. Overhead, the honking moan of migrating geese builds slowly, rolls loud and rowdy over my cottage, then drifts on down towards the nature reserve reservoir a mile away.

For ten or twenty minutes I lie there, mentally mapping the world of old woodland, fields and ponds, and the fish-filled streams that criss-cross the landscape outside. Through a patchwork of cracks in the lath and plaster ceiling, I can hear the bumping scuffle of the resident rats in the roof. Then a wren marks the start of a new day's dawn chorus with a shrill *tic-tic-tic*, and a range of other songbirds join in with their own strange, staccato clicks and popping beeps weaving between the soft oval bassline *hoo-hoo-woo* of wood pigeons.

I feel it before I see it – it's Flash's fault; it's from his fur – the crawling tickle across my skin of a flea shifting at speed suddenly pings off across the room, as Thomas the goshawk begins calling from his mews in the garden.

LAST FLIGHT OF THE GOSHAWK?

We get up and go downstairs. Stepping outside, sipping a mug of hot coffee, I can feel that the temperature drop has a newly refreshed edge, a crisp coldness that holds the thin earthy scent of old bonfire smoke, mud and wet leaves. Over the cut stubble in front of me a small, silhouetted cluster of ducks circles down quacking onto the little sandpit pond. The morning sun's weak warmth touches my skin, almost urging me to begin the circular seasonal ritual that keeps me grounded and living at this location.

*

For me, as a falconer, the freedom of flight, harvesting food, and the natural world are elementally interchangeable – falconry is the nexus that connects all three. For twenty years the simplicity of this equation has given my life meaning and provided a way to explore the natural world.

But for nearly two years Covid has clipped my wings. Like everyone else, I have been instructed by nature to stand down and my movements have been curtailed by the virus. Now the lockdowns have loosened, and the vaccine programme is underway, I am free to fly again, to re-release the six thousand years of collective human knowledge passed on to the world by the tribal nomads who lived on the grassland belts of Mongolia, Kazakhstan and China as far back as 4,000 BCE.

Self-sufficient, highly organised and aggressive, these people were also intuitive, sensitive and expert with dogs and horses. As they travelled across the vast and varied tundra, hunting, gathering, herding and trading, they trapped young hawks and falcons or took them from nests. Applying similar techniques to those they used to train their dogs and horses, they developed the basic skills that would go on to become falconry. Moving and migrating with their birds, through the Altai mountains and down through arid valleys, perhaps resting in villages or gathering in towns for celebrations, they encountered other nomads. Thus the skills of falconry gradually flowed into the network of silk roads that began to stretch out from Persia and the Middle East in the fifth and sixth centuries.

As knowledge of falconry leapfrogged along these supply chains, the birds themselves were traded, bartered, bought and sold by rich merchants and warring men of wealth: warriors, Mongol warlords, khans, crusaders, emperors, Arab princes, emirs, sheiks, sultans, caliphs, kings, queens, and the lords and ladies of Europe all imported, exported or gifted goshawks, sparrowhawks, lanners, sakers, gyr and peregrine falcons, merlins and eagles, as high-value chattels and for the purpose of falconry. Flown and displayed in the elite circles of courts and kingdoms, at large festivals and field meets, birds of prey became part of a vast array of different cultures.

Along with the rat and the flea, hawks and falcons have silently witnessed more events in global human history than perhaps any other non-domesticated animal, including the many infamous examples of viral diseases that have devastated us as a species. In the early thirteenth century, high up on the north-east plains of Mongolia, the descendants of the orig-inal falconer nomads continued to use traditional nets, traps, dogs, goshawks, saker falcons and golden eagles to catch and kill a range of wild animals for food and fur. The fleas in the fur of certain rodent species, particularly giant gerbils and marmots, carry a naturally occurring deadly bacterium in their saliva – *Yersinia pestis*. By the 1340s these fleas had been brought from the Russian steppes by travelling merchants who gathered in marketplaces, and were carried along the now well-established silk roads by rats, dogs and camels, and in food, bedding, bolts of cloth, animal pelts and other commodities.

The cooler environment of the northeast region kept the life cycle of the fleas under localised control. But as they came into contact with warmer weather conditions their breeding behaviour changed, and, rapidly multiplying, they went on to infect a wider variety of humans, among them the soldiers of the Mongol Golden Horde, who in 1344 went west and laid siege to the Genoese trading port of

Caffa on the Black Sea.[1] During a three-year military stalemate outside the city walls, *Yersinia pestis* swept through the Mongol besiegers, killing thousands of men every day. Witnesses wrote of how the Mongol army, forced to retreat, catapulted pustulant corpses over the walls of Caffa in order to kill the Italian merchants who controlled the city. When the Italians fled, the fleas went with them, and in 1347 *Yersinia pestis* passed smoothly into mainland Europe, finally arriving in England in June 1348 in cargoes imported by sailors, and on their ships' rats. Thus the distant people, their food-gathering methods, and the trade routes that gave us falconry, inadvertently unleashed Black Death and bubonic plague, which wiped out millions of humans worldwide, and an assumed 80 per cent of the British population, transforming our culture forever.

When the practice of falconry crossed the Atlantic in 1624, brought to the New World by the English coloniser Thomas Morton, it was still entwined with trade and viral devastation. Morton was America's first falconer, its first nature writer and first satirist, and a key chronicler of the early colonisation of America. In 1637 he published a now very rare, almost unheard-of, book called *New English Canaan*, detailing his time in Massachusetts. In chapter three, 'Of a Great Mortality that Happened Amongst the Natives of New England Near about the Time That the English Came There to Plant', he presents a powerful contemporary testimony of an Old World pestilence arriving in the New World, and the effect it had on the native Wampanoag nation.[2]

Between 1616 and 1618, roughly 122,000 of an estimated indigenous Algonquin population of 150,000 was killed by a virgin soil epidemic thought to have been brought to their shores by French sailors. As Morton walked the Massachusetts landscape, exploring, trapping, and training and flying his falcons, he wrote that the Wampanoag had *died in heaps as they lay in their houses…* [and their] *carcasses lie above the ground, without burial… for crows, kites and vermin to prey upon,* and the *bones and skulls upon the several places of their habitations made such a spectacle* that rather than a New World, it *seemed to me a new-found Golgotha.*[3]

The English merchants who financed colonisation saw it differently, insisting it was by God's divine visitation that *a wonderful plague* had led to *the utter destruction, devastation, and depopulation of that whole territory,* thus clearing the way for the English settlements of the pilgrims at Plymouth in 1620, of Morton at Mount Wollaston in 1624, and of the Puritans of the Massachusetts Bay Company at Boston in 1630.[4]

In part precipitated by a pandemic, and witnessed at first hand by a falconer, this was the birth

of modern America. An event which – like the trans-
ference of *Yesinia pestis* – has conspicuously changed
global human history and the myriad ways in which
we are now forced to relate to our planet.

*

Finishing my coffee, I step back into the kitchen, put
on my hawking jacket, and take Thomas's rewards
from the fridge. Then I check the battery levels of
the radio telemetry trackers, and that the signals
are strong. I slip on my glove and smell the wax,
saddle soap and years of layered leather treatment,
as I follow the dogs up through the garden, dipping
under the bending boughs of several damson trees,
to Thomas's mews.

Inside his mews, my eyes adjust to the obscurity
and shadowed half-light. At first Thomas's chest
feathers throw out a soft luminosity. Registering my
presence, he opens his wings defensively; a second
later, he greets me with a loud sustained scream of
recognition, then throws himself forwards onto the
safety of his high shelf perch. He stares me down,
measuring me up, bobs his aerodynamically-narrow
head and locks on to my deliberately slow movements with his perfectly circular lemon-yellow eyes.
I watch for the physical signs and signals, and when
Thomas visibly softens I reach out to offer him my
glove. He duly steps up trustingly, and his initially

aggressive grip lessens as he adjusts his balance, shuffling about like a delicate featherweight boxer.

Compared to his parents, Thomas is deceptively small, almost elfin-thin, with a sparrowhawk's sleekness – a smoothly tapered two-foot shape that cuts through the air with the understated ease of a perfectly evolved avian predator. Typical of European goshawks, his outer feathers reflect the shaded fractal patterns of the winter forests in which the maternal side of his family evolved. They are an almost infinite variety of dark marbled bark tones crosshatched with liquid-dripping abstract clay browns and creams with thin ochre-yellow edges.

Arthur, his father, has a lineage that stretches back to the subspecies first used by Mongolian falconers on the Russian steppes. As a distant echo and matchless mirror of that environment, the underside of Thomas's wing and tail feathers are a subtle combination of ghostly greys striated with white, which seem freckled with specks of granite, mica and shale, or dusted with pastel-blue quartz.

I carry him out into the open. We push through a gap in the hedge, and I pause on the path to attach the two radio trackers to lightweight brass clips mounted on his tail. Preparing Thomas for free flight and hunting, I remove his leash, swivel and jesses. After the long limitations of the lockdowns, with surprising ease I find myself instinctively switching smoothly into a subtle, unique mindset that has been missing from my life for far too long. My focus in this moment is immense; I feel my senses start to recalibrate through the immediate needs of the hawk into a heightened sensitivity and a level-headed clarity.

The morning light is now blinding bright, and after a heavy rainfall last night the path is slanted with translucent beams of mist that strafe our faces and feathers as I walk. At the bottom of the path, near the noise of the waterfall, I turn right along the edge of a sugar beet field and follow the brook upstream. A hatch of midges floats in pin-prick pulsing clouds, and where the current slackens and slows the water eddies behind exposed roots of alder. Hundreds of pond skaters – like little spiders dancing on ice – pepper the shallow surface, trying not to float off downstream.

When we arrive at the sandpit pond, I lift Thomas high above my head and we slide sideways through dense nettles. The ducks we saw circling earlier suddenly flush, and Thomas lunges forward from the glove. I hold him back and his frustrated flapping shadow scares a pod of carp in the shallows. The water distorts as they bolt away through cold clouds of silt, uprooting the yellowing buried tubers of dead lily pads.

When a modicum of calm is restored, we move along the top of the pond and climb down into a crumbling old stone grotto in search of pheasants. Originally built as a quiet contemplative space for the local parson to write his sermons, it is now no more than a semi-circular wall in the final stages of fragmented entropy, disintegrating and sinking into the soft sand excavated by what was once a healthy and vibrant colony of rabbits.

Two or three seasons before Covid came, a black rabbit arrived here at the grotto, probably a domesticated escapee with a sensible urge to return to her roots and re-wild herself. I was surprised that she survived, and more so in the spring when six or seven multicoloured offspring began hopping about, feasting on the soft crops and fresh growing shoots.

A month later the only evidence that any rabbits had existed at all were small piles of pale desiccated droppings. Nothing was fresh; there were no clusters of dark moist excrement, crops were growing back, and cobwebs now hung across the entrances to the burrows. Occasionally I caught a slight flash of white, or the pointed tops of elongated ears above ground, then nothing – literally hundreds, perhaps thousands, of rabbits had seemingly evaporated.

For years I had watched the manmade barbarity of myxomatosis destroy rabbits in the most visible and inhumane way imaginable. This was different – silent, invisible, unobtrusive, under-reported – and, as I learnt, highly contagious. Rabbit Haemorrhagic

Disease Virus (RHDVa), which kills rapidly, was first reported in Jiangsu Province in China in 1984.[5] By 1985 RHDVa had destroyed upwards of 140 million Chinese domesticated and farmed rabbits. Transmission was said to be through contact with infected offal, meat, fur, flies, fleas and mosquitoes. This allowed the virus to spread westwards along various industrialised meat and fur distribution chains until it entered the United Kingdom in 1992.

In 2010, a new strain was identified in France. Known as RHDV2, it had genetic anomalies which scientists claimed indicated that it had originated from another unknown source rather than being a mutated version of the original virus. Either way, RHDV2 made its way into England in 2014, and was powerful enough to infect and kill vaccinated rabbits and young wild rabbits, and also to leap between species, killing that most mythic and majestic of all lagomorphs – the hare. By this time the worldwide death toll for rabbits was estimated to be in the billions.

It was probably the domestic escapee I had seen that had infected and wiped out the wild populations in the grotto and surrounding land. Thankfully goshawks don't rely on a single food source to survive. So, without really contemplating what this viral intrusion meant, the mechanisms by which it had arrived, or indeed extrapolating its effects outwards towards other creatures let alone humans, we switched to different quarry. Our lives carried on as normal and I left the rabbits to try and re-establish themselves.

In so doing, I observed a fascinating new pattern emerge. Each year, any survivors from the previous year multiply, and at the start of August the young-sters are above ground in significant numbers. But by the end of the month, they are dead. It seems the virus remains prevalent and dynamic in the local eco-system in a darkly clever way. The surviving females carry the antibodies to RHVD2 in their milk, but once the kits are weaned they have a two- or three-week window before their immunity drops and the herpes-like virus kills them. The rabbits' existence is now entirely dictated by the virus's biology; those individuals that succumb to the virus have a short-ened life cycle of weeks or months, not years.

As I move with Thomas away from the rabbit warren and around the old stone grotto, out in the field a light breeze carries the smell of chemicals and a taste in the air akin to acrid warm soap from tonnes of industrial chicken waste, sculpted months ago into a huge mountain of organic fertiliser. A fetid syrupy liquid leaks out like an oil spill from its base. Old straw bedding, blue tissue paper, eggshells, rubber gloves, and the bent feathers scraped from the floors of the factory cages poke through the black cracked solids. Thin grey-stemmed fungi, fine as spun glass, sprout out beautifully in their hundreds. Running between them, a pair of pied wagtails feed on the millions of tiny drosophila-type flies that are themselves feasting on the sloppy glut of food.

Upwind, away from the messy black mass, we take a left turn along a blackthorn hedge. Two hundred yards further on we are able to wade out into a set-aside area of slightly wet grasses, itchy thistles and ragwort full of hopping protein-rich, soft-bodied insects, which also provides protective cover for game birds. I reach down and put a reluctant Flash on his lead. Etta works better here; she flows through low cover and points at anything crouching and secretly hidden. For nearly ten years I have trusted her instincts completely. With almost telekinetic sensitivity, Etta slips forward without command, lifts her head and sniffs, and her posture and breathing transport her to a parallel world of different-shaped scents and various taste-textured forms invisible to me. My anticipation mixes thickly with excitement, my breathing eases into a shallow rhythm, and the expectation mounts higher as Etta continues, persistent and consistent. Her athletic lines are sublime as she scans the land and slows, unsure, then slides delightfully to a point – primed. Twelve feet in front of her the grasses part, and five little red-legged partridge fire high into the sky and scatter with a cackling *kek-kek-kek* alarm call. Thomas reacts instantly, flying hard on a rhythmic wingbeat. In the first second he selects the slowest partridge, and under pressure it momentarily dips in the air. For two more seconds they climb together in a scything flight that disappears over the rusted remains of the roofs on the nearby farm buildings. We eventually find them on the end of a bare patch of ground, silently wedged between a pile of old bricks and a sandstone wall. I crouch down. Beneath Thomas's chest, the dead partridge is tucked up and crushed in his talons, the lightness of its life now translated into a physical ripple of pleasure across the goshawk's feathers. Tentatively I reach in towards Thomas to help break up his kill. His beak is wide open, his tongue pokes out, and I can hear the panting exertion of the flight while I cut into the carcass with the tip of my knife. As I strip out the soft organs with my hand, Thomas sees blood, the fresh wetness; he twitters, excited, and tears at the exposed flesh on his own initiative, then gently takes the food I offer from between my fingers.

Watching Thomas feed, I begin to feel the deep synthesis, balance and inherent celebration of survival that falconry brings. An extension of nature, an instinctive morality where a life gives rise to another fairly and with respect. Yet at the same time I know this moment is only a brief respite on an evolutionary fine line that flows both ways. It was inevitable then that when my turn came in March 2020 and the Covid virus crossed into my system, its presence would force me to contemplate my own mortality rather than that of another animal.

Initially, as the symptoms emerged, I was slightly appalled, yet strangely honoured to be the soft host of a global entity which had passed between species, cultures and continents, and arrived inside my body via the same sort of marketplaces and supply chains as had brought us the art of falconry, as well as *Yersinia pestis*, RHVD and other blood-borne diseases. There were moments when I thought I could sense the virus spreading within, almost feel its gestation and replication, like an internal cellular swarming, or a molecular Golden Horde laying siege in twenty-four-hour cycles to the inner walls of my body. There were phases of dizziness, of lurching sideways in the garden, when I came close to fainting. On another day I had hot flushes and sweating, then there was a day of flu-like fatigue. It was as if the virus was 'thinking', calculating, adjusting its modes of attack, and pushing at the boundaries of my immunity, perhaps scanning me to find a genetic weakness or grading me for selection and death against a biological database of those it had collectively come in contact with or killed. Logically, this was impossible, and I knew it couldn't do those things. Nonetheless, the psychogeography, the feeling that this *may* have been happening, was deeply disconcerting. Ultimately, it felt as though the internal landscape of my own body no longer belonged to me.

On or around day nine, this faintly pretentious, literary self-awareness collapsed when I woke in the pitch dark before dawn, feeling as if someone had dropped a concrete block on my chest. I sat bolt upright, then found myself doubled over, coughing, and alone. It was like drowning in air, and in that moment I felt true vulnerability and became properly scared. This 'thing' was working away within me, and the power of its utter indifference towards my existence was outrageous in the extreme – there were no words, no discussion, no respite, no apologies, no control, no choice, no second chances. If this gets worse, I thought, I am going to die.

I didn't. It peaked and, as with the previous days' symptoms, slowly rolled back and stopped. I caught my breath, relaxed, held the dogs tight, and listened to the exquisite sound of one more dawn chorus before I fell back to sleep.

However, what remained was an uncomfortable residual fear, and fear changes human behaviour. In the wider world, this type of fear, and the relentless mental fatigue caused by both the threat of the virus and repeated lockdowns, seemed to spread further, faster and more corrosively than the virus itself. The irony was that these feelings were apparently only alleviated by the very thing that created Covid in the first place – nature.

I listened to a growing number of radio presenters and their guests discuss the lockdowns, the new-found silence in the sky and on the roads, and how different noises and a new type of thinking were filling the spaces vacated by enforced human inactivity. Articles were written by experts, psychologists, politicians and scientists, analysing the interplay between industry supply chains, climate change, the virus, health and healing, and emphasising that in times of crisis the natural world is fundamental to mental wellbeing and happiness.

Quite quickly the area where I live became a popular place of escape, for curative exercise and re-engagement with the natural world as prescribed by these pundits. Those that visited posted pictures and reviews on social media which went slightly viral, and I suddenly found myself living in one of the top ten places of secretive escape and regeneration in the county.

In a pre-pandemic world, I saw about five people a week. Now upwards of thirty, forty or fifty people were passing within fifteen feet of my front door every day. Set free for their allocated hour, they were smiling, and the atmosphere was at times festive with what I took to be the subconscious celebration of their own survival. Some said hello and we chatted. Often, their conversation slid easily into words of wonder at the world around them, the need for conservation, consideration, and reading the warning signs. Some even expressed the genuine belief that when the pandemic was finished humanity would take a new direction and make changes for the better.

Over time, less welcome were the significant and almost equal number of people who passed through leaving numerous signs of stress, thefts, small deaths and mess. I found face masks, hand wipes, fast-food wrappers, fly-tipped refuse, plastic gel bottles, drink cans, human faeces under hedges, dog-shit bags hung on branches, used nappies and condoms, even an old faux-leather sofa, all just dumped indiscriminately. I saw crushed crops, broken fences, gates left open, poaching from the streams – all of these preceded the inevitable new signs of closure, restriction and defence by those who owned the land.

STRICTLY NO ENTRY!
KEEP OUT!
NO PARKING – ACCESS REQUIRED 24 HRS!
NO TURNING!
PRIVATE PROPERTY!
STAY ON PATHS!
NO PUBLIC RIGHT OF WAY!

BEN CRANE

CLOSE GATES!
NO WILD SWIMMING!
NO FISHING!
NO WALKING!
NO DOGS!

As the polluters and mess makers continued to secretly deplete what others clearly needed to heal, I found myself unable to tell who was who and which were which. For these people there was no new thinking, no new direction, no change for the better, and as the lockdowns dragged on it got worse. Eventually withdrawing into semi-silence, my attitude to those who sought out the restorative powers of nature calcified into a resentful ambivalence towards their presence.

*

At the old stone buildings Thomas continues to feed. I sit back on my haunches and wipe the blood from my hands onto my trouser leg. Far behind Thomas the grey-blue slate tiles of the mansion house of the country estate where I work break through the tree-tops. I become aware of time, and am pulled back by thoughts of a minimum wage and a full day ahead of hard labour in readiness for winter.

I thread on Thomas's jesses and swivel, and once more secure his leash to my glove. Then I pick him up, along with what remains of the partridge, and we begin to wind our way back down towards the brook and home. Crossing a gravel bar and a shallow riffle of water to the opposite bank, we carry on up through the fields and climb the stile. I loop the leads over the dogs' heads and turn left onto a lane without traffic, and a scarcity of people not seen since pre-pandemic days.

At the top of the lane, I pause at a particular spot and recollect the moment my self-righteous indignation towards those who visited transformed into something else entirely. As one among many, a dozen times I passed and purposely ignored the car parked here, until a newly posted 'Police Aware' sticker appeared on the windscreen. On the ground near the passenger door, I saw a fat splatter of chalk-white vomit and a used tissue. Inside, on the seat, were ten to fifteen empty boxes and spent blister packs of generic supermarket painkillers. A half-filled orange sippy cup rested between two child safety seats – Barbie and Spiderman – and a folded-down pushchair. An unknown woman, a mother, had succeeded in killing herself. Had the isolation of lockdown pushed her to a point where not even the purported powers of nature could stop the destruction of her pain?

A week later the car was gone. Not long after it was removed, I re-read Thomas Morton's *New English Canaan*. In the chapters following 'Of *a Great Mortality'*, he describes how in a post-pandemic Massachusetts the Wampanoag revealed to him the ways in which they dealt with their dead. After burial and mourning, '*they absolutely abandon the place, because they suppose the sight thereof will but renew their sorrow*' and '*it was a thing very offensive to them, at our first coming to those parts, to ask of them for anyone that had been dead.*' This was so the deceased could journey to their afterlife without being distracted and called back by name. It was a way of letting go with silent respect, while locating loved ones in personal memory and tying them to a specific location in the landscape.[6]

What that woman could not possibly have known is that the place she chose has for many years been a secret shrine, and the site where I bury my dogs and hawks when they die, a place of personal remembrance and mourning, and of reconciliation and rebuilding after they are gone. It wasn't much, but it was within my power to allow her memory to be absorbed into my secret spot. For me, now, when the abstract numbers of those dead or dying worldwide from Covid have passed beyond comprehension, what remain most vivid are the thought of a despairing mother, and the image of the little orange sippy cup, two empty child seats and a folded down pushchair.

*

LAST FLIGHT OF THE GOSHAWK?

I remove what's left of the partridge carcass from Thomas. He shuffles about on the glove looking for his food, concludes he hasn't been robbed, and relaxes. What little meat is left for me I place in the pocket of my hawking jacket.

Dropping down onto the path opposite the old coppice and my burial site, we cross a concrete bridge near the waterfall and three teal flush from the surface of the stream. Instinctively, Thomas moves to make a kill, and, as with the ducks on the little sandpit pond from earlier, I hold him back and turn to protect him. A minute later, we push back through the gap in the hedge, and come to the far end of our garden.

The sun, higher now, spreads across the top of the hazel hedge. In front of us, strings of light on single strands of spider web criss-cross the trees from one side of the garden to the other. I move through these gossamer silk roads, feeling their slight elasticated tension snapping. Placing Thomas on his perch, I wipe the sticky threads from my arms, face and eyelashes, and reach out to smooth his feathers down. His crop bulges full of fresh meat, and the mud and blood on his chest have dried and darkened to flaky smudges the size of thumbprints.

Using the garden hose, I fill up his bath. For fun, I jam my thumb over the spout and create a flattened misty spray that falls through the sunshine like light rain. Thomas opens his wings inside my mini-rainbow, then looks down at the bath inquisitively. With a quick flapping hop he drops down to the ground. Dipping his beak into the water he tips his head back and sips as a new skein of geese passes above us. We look up at the same time and track their descent over the laurel trees down towards the nature reserve and wildlife sanctuary.

*

I think it is quite possible that, of the various viral pandemics presently surrounding us, the bacillus of the HPAI H5 strain of avian flu is perhaps the prettiest. Unlike Covid and RHVD, this is the viral infection that will probably kill Thomas. It is also the pandemic most likely to lead to the death of falconry in the United Kingdom. In one form or another 'fowl plague' has circulated the earth since it was first recorded in 1878. The strain which we currently live with – A/H5N1 – was originally isolated from a goose in China in 1996, and the spectroscopic image I have pinned up in the cottage shows a rough-surfaced purple spherical cell, with a kaleidoscopic range of translucent rainbow colours over a glowing golden core. It makes me think of a beautiful but malevolent planet.

The first human H5N1 infection was reported in 1997. By 2020, H5N1 had mutated exponentially, and in August 2021 Defra published a report stating, 'The epizootic of HPAI H5 in Europe in autumn/winter 2020/2021 was unprecedented both in the number of neuraminidase (N) subtypes and the number of wild birds affected,' and 'In total, 320 HPAI H5 cases have been reported in wild birds in the UK over the autumn/winter/spring 2020/2021 epizootic.'[7]

The primary vectors for transmission of HPAI are migrating ducks, geese and other wading sea birds. Humans at highest risk of infection are those who handle live birds, come into contact with infected poultry waste, or catch and kill wild birds and eat them. Since the first bird-to-human transmission in 1997 there has been an increase in critical infections and death rates in a range of human hosts. In 2020, the Covid-19 and HPAI pandemics overlapped, and the flying of any falconry birds was effectively banned in order to curtail the spread of an infection which, like Covid and RHDV, ebbs and flows with seasonal highs and lows but shows no signs of abating as it mutates.

New cases of avian flu in swans have already been confirmed in Stratford-upon-Avon.[8] In the next few weeks and months waves of HPAI will spread to Cheshire, Lincolnshire, North and East Yorkshire, Leicester, Hereford, Shropshire, Tyne and Wear, Gloucester, Durham, Derbyshire, Wiltshire,

Cumbria, South Suffolk and Lancashire. On the Solway coast around four thousand barnacle geese will die of HPAI. Other species killed will include pink footed, greylag and Canada geese, common buzzards, red kites, a peregrine falcon, pheasants, rook, great skuas, various gulls, a curlew, whooper swan, great crested grebe, mallard ducks, kestrels, widgeon, a sea eagle, a lapwing, sparrowhawks, grey herons, and thousands of chickens.[9] With a landscape increasingly degraded by human activity, next to no new generational uptake and fewer than a thousand properly dedicated falconers left in Britain, HPAI, Covid and to a degree RHVD mean that those of us who are left are to bear witness to our own demise.[10]

If I lose the freedom to fly Thomas, then I lose something that UNESCO recognises as an intangible, global cultural heritage, with methods and a mindset as legitimate as those of any other indigenous hunting and gathering society.[11]

As with all finely balanced nature-based communities, this loss threatens to destroy the broader complex cultural heritage that has evolved out of such a close connection to the natural world. It means an end to our varied seasonal field meets, dress codes, ceremonies, festivals, travel, folklore, fictions and mythologies, the erosion of falconry's fine art, sculpture, painting, photography, film, writing, songs and music, and of the traditional crafts that create the bells, braiding, specific knots, knives, intricate leashes, jesses, leatherwork, walking sticks, hood designs, gloves, bags and boots.

It would also mean the slow extinction of a living language that bonds diverse human beings through the use of unique hybrid words that possess their own poetry – *creance, bechins, brancher, cadge, chancellere, imp, pelf, petty-singles, imprinting, panels, mantle, yarak, tiercel, austringer, eyas* – and thousands more that have taught me to react empathically to the actions of a wild animal, to build a reciprocal relationship with differing species, and thus unlock a world without which I would be bereft. Bereft of the visceral, delicious pleasure of being so close to a wild creature that I can see my reflection appear across the domed surface of, and within, iridescent eyes that have mesmerised humans for millennia. Or of marvelling at feathers evolved to hairs protecting the nares of the hawk's nose, or the smooth blue-black beak comprised of delicate layers like a shell or the rings of a tree. And the extraordinary oddity of an arrow-shaped lizard-like tongue in a mouth that emits meat-flavoured wet sneezes, or comically flicks away unpleasant-tasting food like an angry toddler. I would miss watching how a hawk yawns, or sniffing and kissing the back of its head, as it stretches its legs, snaps at wasps and flies, shakes its feathers and waggles its tail. I would even miss the skin-piercing pressure of talons, and the erratic rages in the early stages of training – being struck hard, wing-whipped, bitten, footed, attacked, scratched and hurt – while knowing that, with the application of patient concentration and six-thousand-year-old skills, these characteristics will evolve to result in a hawk nibbling my fingers, pulling my hair, or tugging at my shirt cuffs. I would regret bitterly the loss of the trust that underpins the illogicality and unbridled elation of a free-flying animal choosing to return to my glove, and the loss of being an integral part of the art of their performance, of witnessing the limitless aesthetic forms each individual flight takes, even including the way they are free to rake-away, or to fail to return and sometimes remain out overnight – or worse. It means the loss of the intense humility of living face to face with the unpredictable feral grace of nature on a daily basis. Of dealing with short lives lived at high speed. Deaths, though devoid of sentimentality, still command the eloquence of tragedy, and the often-futile high price paid trying to fight illness, injury, and diseases with oddly beautiful nomenclature – *frounce, fillanders, cray, canker, bumble foot, aspergillosis, genetic epilepsy, parasites, coccidiosis, tuberculosis.* And now the viral horror of HPAI, likely secreted in the faeces of the ducks and geese migrating to the safety of the wild life sanctuary well within striking distance of where we now stand.

LAST FLIGHT OF THE GOSHAWK?

Living in such close proximity to nature is always a risk. As history shows, the fragility of all life, the certainty of contagion and deaths, and changing ecosystems have always moved in natural parallel with people and their cultural systems and with wild creatures, and always will.

However, the spread of Covid, RHVD and HPAI is in a sense unnatural. Specifically, HPAI owes its existence primarily to integrated indoor poultry factories, commercial range-raised poultry farms, and live poultry markets. These industrialised systems and supply chains keep bird flu in circulation and leeching into wild migratory networks, which represents the largest factor in the spread of HPAI. Worldwide, HPAI outbreaks continue to arrive, thrive and escalate, as a direct result of increased commercial poultry production since the 1990s.[12]

As with so much else in the present day, the very likely loss of Thomas and the death of falconry is an entirely manmade construct. So what some would applaud as the ending of an inhuman, cruel process speaks of a far deeper and more complex truth.

It is my belief that any productive human life hinges on a coherent sense of identity, one acting in balance with the world. Our inner and outer worlds have to be self-willed and mutually supportive; any schism between the two more often than not ends in destructive crisis.

In the two decades prior to RHDV, Covid and HPAI outbreaks, I travelled to many different continents and countries, talking to and learning from a variety of traditional hunting and falconry communities. The concept of an inner and outer life matched and mirroring nature was expressed in many different ways, by many different cultures, including the last remaining members of the Wampanoag nation.

Visiting them as a falconer, not unlike the way Thomas Morton did in 1624, I asked one young Wampanoag woman how they cope with knowing what the Massachusetts landscape was like before people like Morton arrived compared to how it is now. Her answer was far-reaching and deceptively simple: *'We see ourselves as having a moccasin in one world and a shoe in another. We have a split personality. This is where some of the problems seep in.'*

Without free access to the natural world through falconry, I find my identity weakens and disintegrates in a similar sort of way. It has taken a whole lifetime to comprehend that my pursuit of what I perceive as pure nature is an attempt to maintain my proper state, my natural state. To be active inside nature and not separate – this is the recurring mindset I felt this morning with Thomas; it is the emotion every falconer has felt since the time of the nomads on the Russian steppes.

LAST FLIGHT OF THE GOSHAWK?

Out there in the landscape, out flying, is to collapse any boundaries between myself and the natural world, to feel no sense of enclosure, experience no demarcated rules. I am in the now; I become uncoiled, all my senses receptive to the humming vibration between myself, the hawk, the dog, the earth, air, blood and mud. I feel a definite transformation into the best I can be. This sophisticated and complicated sensation is the primary inspiration for writing, self-expression, self-reflection and self-knowledge. In this context nature is a guiding light, a moral focal point, the only *true* way of measuring myself.

Far from metaphysical primitivism, or quaint animalistic spirituality, I believe this to be concrete and real. There have been many times when I have been without a hawk, existing in an increasingly narrow manmade world where the rules – to me – were illusory and made no real sense. All that seemed to be required was submissive obedience. I existed in a twilight life, dead but living, and the things I distrust about myself were amplified, leaving me fearful and lost – very much like the woman in the car.

Yet these two worlds exist side by side. As I struggle to maintain equilibrium between the two, falconry becomes far more than just killing things to eat; it has its own ecology of freedom.

*

In the garden Thomas begins rolling around happily, flapping his wings in the bath. Like all true forces of nature, he is indifferent to his own far-reaching historic symbolism and the overlapping and inter-connecting meaning I place upon his shoulders. Leaning down to meet him, I join in, scooping up and flicking the fresh water at his chest, head and back. When we finish play-bathing, I lift him up and re-place him carefully on his perch.

However significant the loss of all these things will be, they are inconsequential compared to the loss of the only thing that *really* matters. Due to HPAI it is wholly possible Thomas could be dead within the next twenty-four hours.

Unlike Covid and RHVD there is neither a cure nor viable vaccine for HPAI. Like all wild animals, Thomas will show no symptoms or signs of distress or weakness, until it is too late. Only then will I start to see black haemorrhages and bruises on the shanks of his legs and under his skin. He will stop eating, then suffer respiratory collapse and a hollow snare drum rattling will emerge from his lungs. Within a matter of hours his head will distend, swell, and loll from side to side. His eyes will close to slits, and he will quickly become lethargic and uncoordi-nated. His wings will droop. His legs and feet will lose their power to grip, and in the run-up to death, he will fall from his perch and begin the degradation of seizures and full body fitting on the ground.

I refuse to allow him to undergo such humiliation and suffering. Before any of these things kill him, I will choose to have him euthanised by a vet. I know from experience I will insist on holding him as the first needle is pushed deep into his chest muscle. In my hands he will struggle, lash out with his feet, and make a shrill distressed alarm call. For a minute or more his eyes will be wide and blazing with fear and what seems like confusion. As this initial wave of chemicals slowly shuts down his system, I will hold him close, his body will become floppy, and almost immediately his feathers will dull. The vet will check for a heartbeat while I pointlessly talk to Thomas in a low voice and tell him I am sorry. The vet will apologise as she plucks away at his wing feathers to try and find a vein. Her hands will shake, and when the second injection takes hold his heart will stop, and Thomas will die. The vet will look at me. I will thank her for her kind professionalism, and when she leaves me alone I will pick Thomas up, wrap him in a towel, and he will feel like the heaviest object in the universe.

On the walk to our burial site my pain and rage will be amplified by the knowledge that the price of his life is £67.43 in vets' fees, and whatever immoral profits people make from the industrialised farming of cheap chicken for mass consumption.

*

In the cottage I put what remains of the partridge in the fridge and feed Etta and Flash. I walk back down the lane and across the fields to work. At the machine shed I load up my tools in the little 4x4 and drive with the dogs to the furthest, most isolated corner of the old woodland surrounding a long shallow estate lake.

Following the contours and frail evidence of the old earth paths which were once here, for months I have been delicately reclaiming unobtrusive trails that switch back and forth through the tangled mass of bramble, bamboo and nettle banks. Working away with a rhythmic cutting and shaping of brush, I think about what it is I want to write, allowing discursive set pieces, different viewpoints, and our mornings journey to jostle for position in my mind.

As the bare bones of a loose narrative begins to slowly appear, this is when the reality of my situation reveals itself. However I turn around the various themes of life, death and the cyclicality of the natural world, I arrive at the same dead end. Whatever I describe will be the first public writing about the death of falconry by one of the few full-time falconry writers left in the United Kingdom. This will be nature writing as part celebration, part obituary and part historical document.

LAST FLIGHT OF THE GOSHAWK?

I look at the orange beech and mouldy green horse chestnut leaves littering the surface of the lake. Waterlogged, some begin to fold over and sink, leaving little grooves as they bump along the layered sediment below. I pick at the blackened blood of the dead partridge from under my fingernails. I start to imagine the flow of my own blood and the sound of my heart beating. For a brief moment I feel like the last human left alive on the planet, and although I know death is an inevitable fixed position, life is mutable and keeps moving. I have to hold tightly to the fact that at this precise moment the end is not *now*. Unlike the woman in the car I have today and hopefully tomorrow, while falconry has survived the stratagems of Mongol warlords, shifting supply chains, pestilence, plagues and even the Black Death. Like the rabbits', the cycle of my life has changed, but I am alive and surviving three different types of global pandemic. I have words for self-expression. I have Etta and Flash. I have the privilege of Thomas, who I know is on his perch preening and perfecting his flight feathers, beneath which thin capillaries and veins are carrying his own bright red blood, a wet fire burning within him – ready to begin again. To keep going. To keep flying with a feral grace that is the pathway towards a whole ecology of freedom.

JOANNA POCOCK

NONE OF THIS SHOULD BE HERE

STORY ONE

We arrived in the evening and went straight to the El Cortez, where we'd booked a room. I was not prepared for the lights, the noise, the pinging, the simulated sound of coins coming down a metal chute, the *Ghostbusters* theme tune inexplicably clanging out at regular intervals, the crowds with their plastic buckets of change feeding the machines, the lack of windows and clocks, the stale air.

The image from the El Cortez casino that is seared in my mind is this: a woman in a motorized wheelchair wears a credit card attached to her wrist with what looks like an old telephone cord. The card is permanently stuck in the machine like a baby's pacifier. She is aggressively pumping the arm of the slot machine as money is being sucked from her bank account. Her losses appear to be infinite.

After crossing the casino floor and walking up a couple of flights of stairs, my husband Jason and I found our room. The leaking air conditioning unit had created a small damp patch in the carpet, which was edged with black mould where it met the wall. The window wouldn't open and everything smelled of cigarette smoke. But it was the flickering yellow lighting that undid me. Normally, I can do crappy hotels – in fact I quite like them – but because this was Vegas, where you are supposed to have FUN, I couldn't do it. I left the room, ran down the stairs, walked through the casino, back to where we'd left our rental car and collapsed in a sobbing heap. The valet looked at me, then at Jason, and asked almost sarcastically, 'Is she OK?' I sort of loved him for that.

The only words I could get out were, 'This shouldn't be here. None of this should be here!'

We contemplated driving to LA that night but it was late and we were tired. We found another room at the slightly less melancholic Sahara where we spent the night being cold to each other. Me, unable to verbalise why I had reacted the way I had. Jason, pissed off that his pre-wedding surprise of taking me to Vegas had so spectacularly failed. I felt guilty and he had every reason to be angry. We left Vegas the following morning.

STORY TWO

Three years later, I was back in the city working on a documentary with Jason. We arrived in early spring. It was chilly the night we landed – a desert cold that hit sharply as we stepped onto the tarmac at McCarran Airport. We booked into the Motel 6 on Tropicana, where we didn't have to walk through the maze of a casino to get to our room; we could drive up to our front door, which was a relief. After about a week at the motel, we found an even cheaper room in an Americas Best Value Inn & Suites on South Maryland Parkway. The apartment block was aiming for bland, corporate clientele, but judging from the shouting and the regular appearances by the police, they weren't hitting their target demographic. Everything smelled of air freshener and bedbug spray.

One of the people we were filming was a young woman who had escaped an abusive home and had hitchhiked to Vegas from somewhere in California. She'd been picked up on the highway by a much older guy called Robert, who had invited her to move in with him. They asked us over to their house for a drink so Jason could interview the young woman. They lived in one of those cream-coloured L-shaped bungalows with metal siding, so familiar to me. It was a tract house, a cookie-cutter home like something from a Robert Adams photograph. The streetlights, the sidewalks, the rows of tidy bungalows facing each other across a newly paved street – they all just ended where the desert began. Although this harsh juxtaposition was disturbing, I could somehow understand it. I could put it into a human context of habitation because it seemed transparent and, more importantly it was honest.

No one was trying to hide the ugliness or make it *fun*. It was just there being itself.

This extreme interface between the built-upon and the wild recalled a passage from the influential 1966 book *Learning from Las Vegas*: 'Beyond the town, the only transition between the Strip and the Mojave Desert is a zone of rusting beer cans,' the authors wrote.[1] Yet, here were no rusting beer cans. Here there was only air and the lemony yellow glow of the streetlights where tiny moths danced in suspension. When such an exquisite and fragile landscape butts up against the cheap, fast and ugly man-made environment it creates a kind of melancholia. The lack of humility and understanding in our human encroachment into nature recalled the journalist and cultural critic H. L. Mencken's words, that there exists in America, a 'lust for the hideous, the delight in ugliness for its own sake.'[2]

I did not collapse into a heap of sobbing during this trip in 2005 because I was there to be part of Jason's exploration of Vegas; I was there as an observer. Through this act of mediation, I was able to objectively see a version of Vegas I was beginning to understand. We were not living in the post-modern town described in *Learning from Las Vegas*, nor were we engaging with the city ironically, as a joke, as a flimsy cardboard cut-out, a Pop Art construction, the wet dream of populist pleasure makers, or a simulacrum of a city. I could and I still can appreciate the 'messy vitality' and the unselfconsciousness of the Strip the authors of *Learning from Las Vegas* exalt. I was also aware that this city is a place where people live, work, write poems, worry about their lack of exercise and their kids' college fees. And, yet, besides all this, I simply couldn't – and still can't – shake my view of Las Vegas as human folly, a mistake, an aberration, and most importantly an environmental catastrophe.

The aesthetic of this city, where replicas are visited instead of the real thing, where the trash at the New York, New York casino is collected in garbage trucks disguised as yellow cabs, where signs and signifiers dissolve, fall apart, collide or merge into each other, is an aesthetic that requires some distance, some objectivity to make sense of it. Although being an observer helped me see the city properly, I could not discard my initial visceral response. There should not be an all-you-can-eat seafood buffet in the middle of the desert. A cheeseburger should not weigh fifteen pounds and aquifers and rivers should not be depleted so that fountains outside casinos can jet hundreds of feet into the air all day, every day without end. How can we have fun when we are being invited to partake in ecocidal madness? *This shouldn't be here. None of this should be here.*

NONE OF THIS SHOULD BE HERE

A STORY OF CAKE

The spring and summer that Jason and I were living in Vegas, coincided with the hundredth anniversary of what some referred to as the 'founding' of the city in 1905. 'Founding' is a strange word, because the place had been the home of Southern Paiutes and other indigenous people for hundreds of years. The Spanish named the settlement 'Las Vegas' or 'The Meadows'. Drawn by a spring-fed creek – the only fresh water for miles – Mormons built an adobe fort here. Part of it is still standing, and in 1999, it was turned into a state park. But 1905 has stuck as the year of the city's birth because that was when the railway came to town.

Birthday celebrations had been brewing for months, culminating in the baking of the biggest cake in the world. The seven-layer, 130,000-pound vanilla cake measured 102 feet long, 52 feet wide, and contained 23 million calories. On the day of the great cake slicing, Jason and I lined up outside Cashman Center, a large building like a cross between a storage facility, convention centre and a high school gym. We were with Matt, one of the people Jason had been filming. He was a very quiet and thoughtful gambling addict who'd been rejected by the Mormon Church for falling in love with a non-Mormon. He was currently homeless and often slept in one of the city's storm sewers or in the Salvation Army shelter, when they had a bed.

Thousands of people had shown up clutching Tupperware, cardboard boxes, battered suitcases, even garbage bags to lug their slabs of cake back to their kitchens, offices and rented rooms. We shuffled our way inside where a volunteer in a spattered apron handed us each a slice on a paper plate with a plastic fork stuck in it like a small pitchfork. The three of us found a spot outside in the shade of a tree and watched people leave the Center with as much cake as they could carry. The scene was like a demented children's picnic, art directed by Tim Burton. The planners of this birthday celebration, however, had wildly overestimated how many Las Vegans would want to queue up in 100-degree heat for free cake. On that evening's news, I watched in horror as dump truck after dump truck brought mountains of left-overs to a local pig farm where it was shovelled into their pens for the animals to eat. If there were ever a film clip needed to illustrate America's love of overabundance and extreme levels of waste, this news bulletin would be a strong contender.

In the months that Jason and I were living in Americas Best Value Inn & Suites on South Maryland Parkway, I got pregnant and had a miscarriage. We had been filming on the roof of a multi-storey car park in the beating sunshine when I began to feel light-headed. The temperature had risen to about 115 degrees Fahrenheit that day, and for the past few weeks my morning sickness had been exacerbated by this extreme, unabated heat. We were driving back to our apartment when I felt the sickness disappear. I realised I was somewhere around my ninth week of pregnancy – a danger point my body knew well. Just like that, a switch had been flipped inside me. We ordered pizza to our room and for the first time in almost three months, I felt hungry. The next day I bled and bled and didn't leave the apartment. The swiftness of it all somehow suited the hot, shiny, hardness of the city. *None of this should be here.*

A STORY OF WATER

Consumption is one of the engines fuelling the Vegas that many go there to experience. We have the facts about the environmental cost of this consumption. We know about the extraction of resources needed to make the place hum, sing and glow and we know about the garbage and how most of it ends up in landfill or incinerated, creating clouds of toxic smoke. The year Jason and I were living there, the hotels, casinos and restaurants alone were creating over half a million tons of garbage a year – enough to fill an American football field ten metres high every day.[3] Like all built environments in the American West, you cannot talk about Vegas without mentioning the key ingredient to its very existence: water. When I think about Nevada, my mind immediately moves towards the hundredth longitudinal meridian first observed and then described by John Wesley Powell in his 1878 'Report on the Lands of the Arid regions of the United States'. This line runs from the Canadian border in the north to the Gulf of Mexico in the south, hugging the western edges of Minnesota, Iowa, Missouri, Arkansas and Louisiana. Powell had been commissioned by the government to explore the western territories and see if it were viable to continue handing out 160-acre parcels for farming and homesteading in the West.

After years of travelling, Powell argued that due to its aridity – the West receives on average less than twenty inches of rain per year – it was almost a separate country from the East. A lack of fresh water and rainfall would not sustain high levels of population or intensive agriculture. The government ignored him, and ever since, precious waterways across the West have been dammed, reshaped, exploited and poisoned in the service of progress, extraction and development.

The vast Colorado River, the major waterway in the West and Southwest, became the irrigation source for cities and communities springing up in the desert. Its water was so in demand that in 1922 something called the Colorado River Compact was created which essentially divided the river into two parts. States to the north, Colorado, New Mexico, Utah and Wyoming would be allocated 7.5 million acre-feet of river water a year; while California, Arizona and Nevada another 7.5 million acre-feet plus a million extra. In order for this to happen, the Colorado would need to be dammed. This is where the Hoover Dam comes in with its creation of Lake Mead. This body of water is called a 'lake' but really it acts as a reservoir and a site for recreation. When you come upon Lake Mead, you can tell this large sheet of blue water is out of place. It clashes sharply with the pink rocks that hold it. At least four million people rely on Lake Mead for their water. Famously there is now a 'bathtub ring' running around the rocks that contain it, showing how much the water level has dropped in recent years.

After years of serious drought, the golf courses that dot the desert in and around Vegas have started waking up to the problem of keeping their lawns green. An article appeared recently in the Las Vegas Review-Journal headlined 'New golf courses that come to Las Vegas won't be able to use Colorado River water for irrigation'. The author writes, 'On average, golf courses in Southern Nevada consume 725 acre-feet – about 236 million gallons – every year. One acre-foot is about what two Las Vegas

Valley homes use over the course of 16 months.'[4] Probably the most upsetting fact in all this waste is that most of 'the water used at golf courses is used for irrigation or lost to evaporation and cannot be returned to Lake Mead'. Just like that, this precious resource is left to disappear into thin air.

Nowhere in the coverage of this issue is there a mention of the sacredness of water, its necessity in the existence of all life forms, its place in the mythology of these lands and of our responsibility to protect it. Nothing manages to shift those words I first uttered when I fled the El Cortez Motel and crumpled in a heap. *None of this should be here.*

A STORY OF GARBAGE

The MGM Grand, built in 1973, got its name from the 1932 film *Grand Hotel*, the one where Greta Garbo huskily announces that she wants to be alone. Back then, with its 2,100 luxury rooms, the MGM was the largest hotel in the world. It is still one of the largest casino-hotels in town and it generates so much garbage, that staff there work eight-hour shifts twenty-four hours a day to sort it. Like many other hotels and restaurants in this town, it never stops producing waste, not even for one second.

For places whose meaning revolves around spectacle, the stakes need to be constantly upped, and Vegas is no exception. In 1989, the Mirage hotel appeared with its simulated outdoor Volcano. I've watched queues of people stand and wait for it to erupt as if waiting for the Old Faithful geyser in Yellowstone to blow its boiling water a hundred feet into the air. When the natural is treated as spectacle and when spectacle is created to simulate the natural, I feel as if material reality is coming apart at the seams. I have also seen Siegfried and Roy's white tigers in glass cages inside the Mirage lobby and felt sick to my bones as I watched them pace in their temperature-controlled prisons. They shouldn't be here. *None of this should be here.*

A STORY OF EXPLOSIONS

The Mojave Desert has been blown up, blasted and poisoned by the US military since the first aerial atomic bomb was detonated there in 1951 in a dry lakebed called Frenchman Flat. I took a look on Google maps at the proximity of Frenchman Flat to the Vegas Strip. Google will not give driving directions, but they do tell you that on foot it is 158 miles and would take fifty-two hours to walk. There is also inexplicably a tourist review of Frenchman Flat. 'Not the best hiking spot,' it reads. 'Felt nauseous for some reason and now I'm slowly losing my hair. Would not recommend.'

The famous Nevada Test Site (now rebranded as the Nevada National Security Site), in which

Frenchman Flat sits, is about an hour's drive from the Vegas Strip and occupies an area slightly larger than Rhode Island. Over forty years, almost a thousand nuclear bombs have been detonated there. The last one in 1991 was an underground atomic blast called the 'Divider'. This land that has been bombed and filled with poison belongs to the Western Shoshone – a fact often overlooked when people talk about the Atomic Programme.

The Treaty of Ruby Valley was signed between the Shoshone people and the American government in 1863. It stipulated that the tribe would continue to own the land, but in the words of Ian Zabarte, the Principal Man of the Western Bands of the Shoshone Nation, this would be 'in exchange for $5,000 a year for twenty years, paid in cattle and other goods.'[5] The US would also be allowed to 'establish military posts on the land' and 'mine for minerals on it'. Zabarte was born in 1964, a year after above-ground testing of nuclear weapons was banned. The US, however, continued to test weapons of mass destruction, they just did so underneath his ancestral lands and at the rate of one bomb almost every three weeks. It is hard to imagine the amounts of nuclear fallout that have rained down on these lands, but one comparison is this: the bomb dropped on Hiroshima in 1945 created 13 kilotonnes of nuclear fallout;

whereas between 1951 and 1992 nuclear testing on Shoshone land created 620 kilotonnes.[6] In a 2020 article Zabarte wrote for *Al Jazeera*, he lists the people he knows with cancer – some of whom are toddlers. 'Every family is affected,' he writes. 'I watched my uncle suffer from horrible cancer that ate away at his throat and my grandfather die of an autoimmune disease that is known to be caused by exposure to radiation. They say he had a heart attack, but when your skin falls off, that puts stress on your heart.'[7] The list of friends and family getting sick and dying goes on.

Despite denials from the US Atomic Energy Commission (AEC), incriminating documents were discovered in 1978 in the state archives of Utah, which was downwind from the atomic testing in Nevada. These documents showed that 18,000 sheep were grazing only a few miles to the north and east of the borders of the Nevada Test Site in the early 1950s. None of the ranchers or shepherds were alerted to any dangers before bombs were tested and their concerns since have mostly been dismissed. In 1979, *The New York Times* reported that after grazing in Nevada, 'the sheep were returned to Utah in the spring of 1953' where 'ranchers noted that many were sick and dying. Ewes had spontaneous abortions and showed burn-like lesions on the face, neck and ears.

The majority of lambs were born dead and stunted, and ewes died either during lambing or a few days later, according to the documents.' None of this was enough to convince the AEC that these illnesses and deaths were the result of atomic testing. Even two autopsies that showed the concentration of Iodine 131 – a radioactive isotope – in their thyroid glands exceeded 'by a factor of 250 to 1,000 the maximum permissible concentration of radioactive iodine for humans' was not enough to convince them to compensate the people of these lands for the increased numbers of cancers and other illnesses in their animals and loved ones.[8] Court cases for reparations are still ongoing.

Deserts are fragile and irreplaceable ecosystems, where important cultural, historical and ecological evolution has been taking place for millennia, and yet deserts also function as the sites for our worst and most crazed levels of devastation and desecration. Deserts, to many people are great big nothings, and are often giant blank spaces on maps, yet to the humans, non-humans, and all living things who have acclimatised to these lands for thousands of years, deserts are home, they are a refuge. 'To say nothing is out there is incorrect,' writes the Osage-American author William Least Heat-Moon, 'to say the desert is stingy with everything except space and light, stone and earth is closer to the truth.'[9]

NONE OF THIS SHOULD BE HERE

A STORY OF BURIALS

On federal land, adjacent to the Nevada Test Site sits Yucca Mountain. I say 'federal land' because that is what it is called in Washington. Really, this is also Shoshone land. In 1987, Congress decided that this is where America's nuclear waste would be stored, deep underground. Yucca Mountain, like any place designated to house lethal amounts of nuclear waste was a compromise. There were supposed to be two nuclear repositories in the US – one in the East; one in the West. Politicians in the East complained that there were too many people there to make it viable. So the underpopulated West won the nuclear waste lottery, partly because the state of Nevada, despite the existence of Las Vegas, has a low population. Where to store nuclear waste is always a headache for politicians. Dumping garbage that could essentially kill your constituents is not a vote winner. In 1989, the state of Nevada enacted legislation to make it illegal to store high-level radioactive waste there. For twenty years, this battle over Yucca Mountain has been raging. In 2002, under President Bush it was given the go-ahead, only for it to be halted under President Obama. Meanwhile electricity customers in the US continue paying their bills, some of which contribute to a nuclear waste fund, which has already collected $22 billion. Like so much to do with the environment, the problem has not gone away, it has merely been put on hold.[10]

It will be thousands of years before this waste will be safe to handle or even get close to. Despite the arguments around where it should be buried – barrels of it have already gone into the oceans, while some decision-makers believe we should blast it into space – there is also a hotly contested issue around the 'Danger' sign needed at the entrance to any nuclear burial ground. The classic nuclear logo might not be recognised by our descendants who may be walking the Earth thousands of years from now. How do you make them understand that something is too dangerous to touch? What languages will they speak? What symbols will they recognise? How much knowledge will they have of things like half-life, nuclear contamination, and the ensuing diseases from such materials? Will humans even be around then? Art, architecture and design competitions have been organised in the hopes that we can create symbols, hieroglyphics, plaques, monuments, or pieces of land art which will be able to communicate with humans ten thousand years from now.

In 2017, an architectural design company called 'arch out loud', which brands itself a 'platform for exploring the possibilities of architecture and design... to create innovative solutions for issues facing our world' hosted a competition for a marker to go at the entrance of nuclear waste sites that would be understood by our human descendants thousands of years from now.[11] The winner, 'Testbed', was a site-specific piece that transformed the area into 'an experimental field of climate engineering that manipulates the geology of the site itself by setting in motion an open-ended assemblage of processes that generate an entangled scientific earthwork of hybrid formations.' The runners up were called 'A crystalline funeral', 'A Storm is Blowing From Paradise' and 'Lodestar'. These earthworks might all be wondrously innovative and perhaps they will deter some humans, although I find that idea questionable. And what about the living beings who don't read and write? The plants, the animals, the very soil itself? How will they be protected?

Andra, a French company that designs, develops and operates solutions for radioactive waste, states on their website that the Nuclear Safety Authority rules from 1991 provide for 'the conservation of the repository memory, making it extremely unlikely that human intrusion into the repository area is to be found.'[12] Andra also admits, however, that no one 'can predict whether the organizations today responsible for radioactive waste repositories will still exist in several centuries'. Because of this, 'measures are then put in place so that the memory of these centers lasts as long as possible.' Interestingly, they state that the most efficient means of transmitting the information around nuclear waste burial is to use words on paper – not just any paper, but paper 'first produced in the 1950s ... created from pure cellulose that can be stored for a long time, unlike ordinary paper which deteriorates over a few decades. ... The existence of a storage center must also be anchored in the collective memory. ... The memory of such a site must be shared with its environment, particularly its residents, from generation to generation.'

Creating memories of a site for people who do not yet exist. Surely this is one of the strangest human environmental projects yet. Meanwhile, the real collective memories of indigenous people and their connections to this land and their methods of successfully stewarding it, are being wiped away like an inconvenience. Isn't it odd that we are attempting to develop an oral tradition, one that is devoid of creation myths and moral tales and human beings, while focusing on warning future generations of the poisons we have lodged deep inside the Earth that might kill them?

Gone are the days when the Rat Pack and fellow cocktail drinkers would watch the atomic testing from the roof of a casino as a form of harmless entertainment. During the 1950s, Vegas promoted what it called 'Atomic Tourism'. The bombs were always detonated at dawn and guests would stay up all night and have their final highball with the sunrise and a bonus nuclear blast in the background. Gone also are the bikini-clad women who jostled for the title of Miss Atomic Bomb, the winner being dressed in a bathing suit with ruffles up the front emulating the famous shape of a mushroom cloud. Yet, you can still experience a simulacrum of all this in the National Atomic Testing Museum where for a few dollars you can experience your very own simulated atmospheric bomb blast or learn how to survive an atomic explosion by going beyond the basic 'duck and cover' position.

Atomic tourism may be in the past, and yet we are still living in the Atomic Age. We don't need the fallout to be simulated, because it is all around us. There are maps showing the trail of fallout across the continent from the testing in Nevada. Nowhere is untouched. Those who are still alive and who grew up downwind of the bomb blasts – the 'downwinders' as they're called – those who work in nuclear facilities, those whose land was occupied to make way for atomic testing do not need any of this simulated for them because they are living with the cancers, the deaths and the birth defects. The Atomic Age is less of a spectacle or a beauty pageant and more of a slow, poisonous drip, drip, drip.

JOANNA POCOCK

A STORY OF GENTRIFICATION

It took returning to Vegas alone in 2006 to unpick my initial reaction to the place. To put it in the context of a kind of 'ground truth' – as a visceral response to a place based on observable, or even invisible, information. In my case this ground truth manifested physically. Riding in a gondola in the Venetian is quantitively but not qualitatively different from watching atomic blasts from a casino rooftop. They both spring from the human urge to destroy the Earth. Sinking a Mojito at the Wynne or playing the slots at the Bellagio is an act of participation in this destruction. For me having 'fun' in Vegas is a problem. For me, *none of it should be here*. And that includes me.

The first entry in my journal on my third visit to Vegas in 2006 was written in the Art Bar on Main Street. I had stopped in Vegas as part of a solo Greyhound bus trip across the US. I was escaping a trail of miscarriages, the death of my sister, and I was also writing a novel whose protagonist goes to Vegas to meet her mother. I knew my way around town after my two previous visits and was able to navigate the Downtown and the Arts District. This little area with its small craftsman bungalows – what they called 'cottages' – the second-hand clothing and furniture shops, the graffiti, the mannequins on the sidewalk in feather boas and leather jackets, the galleries, bars and car repair shops – these were all recognisable to me. It wasn't the Vegas of the Strip, nor was it the Vegas of tract housing. It was something else entirely, more like the student neighbourhood of a college town.

I was staying at the Bridger Inn Hotel at the top of Main Street, which was lined with motels in various states of decay. It was like a kinetic museum of collapsing mid-century motel architecture. I could envision the piles of leases in back rooms not being renewed, the contracts left unsigned and the real estate being sold off to developers. Gentrification was in the ether of the Vegas of 2006.

The Art Bar would not have looked out of place in Hackney or Brooklyn. The red velvet sofas, the bust of Elvis, the paintings of James Brown and Aretha Franklin channelling the palette of de Kooning. It was dark and the airwaves were pounding out very loud Eminem. I ordered a Corona with a slice of lime and settled in to write in my journal. The TV was on above the bar. The sound had been muted, but subtitles ran along the bottom. A brunette with a Barbiesque figure walked into an office. She sat next to a shiny and somewhat presidential desk. She picked up what I thought was a jellyfish. We were not entering the realm of Dadaism, however. The jellyfish turned out to be a silicone breast implant. A man entered the room to join her, but he took the big chair behind the desk. It turned out that he was a plastic surgeon and she was his wife and he had done dozens of surgeries on her and she was thrilled about every single nip, tuck, boob job and fat extraction. They were now choosing a new pair of breasts for 'fun'. No one else had been watching the TV. The other customers were having a good time, chatting and laughing. I drank my beer and headed out.

I can't help but wonder what cities would look like if we applied some of the wildlife ecologist Aldo Leopold's 'land ethic', to them. Cities decay, but forests evolve (if we let them). Rivers can run dry or burst their banks, deserts can expand or contract. Nature is fluid and responsive, and yet cities so often seem to go in one direction, they follow the path of the money and become gentrified or they fall apart. Perhaps it is nature's ability for renewal that keeps us gravitating towards it for a sign of how to live well on the planet. By 'well' I mean in a constant harmonious state whereby we take what we need and give back to the Earth what it needs. Aldo Leopold called on humans to recognise that we are members of a 'biotic team' and that we should act in ways that 'preserve the integrity, stability, and beauty of the biotic community'.[13] Surely cities can also be seen as biotic communities. 'We can be ethical only in relation to something we can see, feel, understand, love, or otherwise have faith in,' Leopold wrote. Our ability to reframe our ideas of urban spaces existing as something we can see, feel, understand and love seems at once impossible and yet crucial to the continuation of human and nonhuman life on our planet. The sense of regeneration found in the natural world is in direct contrast to the knowledge that even the tallest, most expensive skyscraper or casino will one day fall and will, over time, become dust. We should be building cities that say, *This should be here.*

I have a dream one night at the Bridger Hotel: I am rolling around in a white room. My nose begins to bleed and I am spattering blood all over the pristine white walls. I want it to stop but I can't stem the bleeding. When I wake, my first thought is about death. Then I realise that blood is also life. This dream is about childbirth. There is so much death in Vegas. The death that comes with not thinking about the Earth. It's time for me to get back on the Greyhound and carry on with my trip.

When I left Vegas, I was reminded of the feminist philosopher and author Simone de Beauvoir's sadness at leaving America after her lecture tour there in 1947. She writes: 'Yes, I believe that this is what moves me so strongly at the moment of my departure: America is one of the pivotal points of the world, where the future of man is being played out. ... It is a battlefield, and you can only become passionate about the battle it is waging with itself, in which the stakes are beyond measure.'[14] It is indeed a pivotal point of the world. It is at times a battlefield. The arguments over water, nuclear waste, the burning of fossil fuels, the extraction that keeps the American way of life humming along and its conflict with indigenous rights – these are all arguments being played out around the world.

During my Greyhound bus trip, as my fellow passengers and I stopped in cities, edgelands, highways, gas stations, seedy motels and parking lots, I rarely saw battles being played out. There was care and kindness among my fellow travellers. Strangers slept in seats next to each other on the bus, people chatted about their problems or bought food for the kids whose parents didn't have quite enough change. There were sunsets and sunrises and little clouds of sand and sagebrush being whipped up in windy deserts across New Mexico, Arizona, Nevada and Texas – or indeed anywhere that there is sand and sagebrush and wind. There were people laughing and there were real life connections happening. Our Greyhound stopped to refuel somewhere between Vegas and Los Angeles. Unlike most of the parking lots we pulled into, this one was badly lit, almost completely dark. Life had conspired to bring me to a patch of desert under a shroud of black sky. I looked up and saw a trail of thousands, millions of stars above me. I was staring at deep time, at burning balls of gas that no longer existed but whose light I could now see. *This should be here.* All of this should be here. This is what I said.

NEHA SINHA

CITY OF COVID-TREES

NEEM

The day I had to leave for the hospital with Covid-19 flaming through my veins, was the day I noticed the first cream-black butterfly land gently on cream flowers. The Neem tree outside my kitchen window was a queen wearing thousands of flowers. This butterfly was Neo, the number one, the first migratory *Belenois aurota* of the season, and I was not going to be around to see the rest.

I will return, I told the butterfly. In the way of butterflies, it was gone already. I wanted to believe what I was saying, and because the Pioneer was gone, I told *Azadirachta indica*, the Neem tree, instead.

The Neem tree has a complex brown bark riven through with lines. I imagine these to be lines of worry because the tree seems to care for all of us. It is so useful and medicinal that its presence in our lives verges on the boring. Snapped-off twigs are used as formerly alive toothbrushes, their bitter taste and young flesh swishing in the mouth like an aperitif. The pinnate leaves are used to treat injuries, create antibacterial baths, wash faces, and even chase away insects from cupboards. Today, it was I getting chased from home towards hospital, a sick family in tow. The Neem stood its ground, its root-feet unwavering.

In the hospital, I was rootless. There was no bed for us. Under a Banyan in the hospital complex, we waited in an ambulance, a litter of strengthening juices, mismatched charging cables, and ammunition strips of medicines heaped around us. People shouted. People cried. The ground was patted down with thundering footsteps – urgent, shoving, crying, meant to save lives. In a wheelchair, my ward sagged. *Can't breathe.* Those were the two words he had said to me a day and a half ago, the last words he had spoken since. The words seemed suspended around our heads like seeds – purposeful, urgent, but likely to be dashed to hopelessness on the unyielding concrete. The wait for the bed stretched on, a drum skin thrumming painfully with tension. In the end, we got the bed because someone had died.

Within the hospital, one learned how to wear *a* mask. Even a collection of masks on the body is called a mask. 'I am wearing a mask,' I say, or: 'I am masked.' This does not reveal the sequence, nor the sheer number of fabrics chafing, jostling and hustling around our collective *can't breathes* in the world's most polluted city. First came the surgical mask, tight, uncompromising, looped around the ears. Then, a cotton mask secured around the ears, whimsical, handloomed, because you don't want to lose yourself in a tidal wave of colourless surgical fabric. Then, a visor, around the forehead, and strapped behind the head. Spectacles with no power, to protect the eyes. As 2020 had merged into 2021, the days merged into each other. Only the number of masks had changed, each trailing with a ghost-mask that would become garbage – from use to refuse, from life-giver to animal life-choker. My head kept playing *can't breathe can't breathe* – the words I had heard, but also emanating from the choked raggedness of my own lungs. I was a patient on the eleventh day of my own infection. And I was also the caregiver.

There were never enough of us to go around.

My brother hovered around me, a twin to my pain. We counted the hours watching each other. There was no place to sit. We stood, we leaned, we lay, we entwined. My ears were sore from mask-elastic. This was a new kind of pandemic discomfort. Our ears are like leaves, I thought, tender but there. Our ears are like Neem leaves I can no longer smell. What do the earless do to fight Covid?

The first time I left the ward was nighttime. I was not trying to get away. There was no dramatic flourish of escape. There was a quieter need to be alone. To weep. To fully feel unrooted for a little while longer while providing shade and sustenance as a caregiver inside the hospital. There were two kinds of energies inside the premises. One: the regimented doctor, resident-doctor and head-doctor energy, whiplashed with cold fury at the unfairness of the human tragedy around them. Two: the unhinged energy of the patients and their relatives, rising in falcon gyre-crescendos from various parts of the hospital. Going through them was like walking in a field of fungus. I didn't know the nature of the beast: if I would be infected with poisons or viruses, or whether it would be as unexpectedly tender as mushroom-skirt frills. I had walked in on a woman peeing in the middle of a corridor that day. I had seen a man wrap himself like a vine around his ward, supporting her as she tried breathing with Covid lungs and a diabetic body. My elastic-scraped leaf-like ears had heard sobs two days running. I wanted aloneness. I wanted de-hysteria. I wanted to rub my ears off.

As I stepped out, a guard slid to me. 'Don't go,' she hissed. 'Your patient's bed will get taken.' It was an odd twilight conference – two women, faceless in masks, railing against a city that is casually called a rape capital. I will be back, I breathed, thankful for her fellow feeling and hating her practicality.

I walked. There were other caregivers, lying in no particular shape around me. The scents I couldn't smell were a marked presence in my consciousness. I walked over the concrete and around the sadnesses. Had I come to die here, or to lie here? I wasn't sure.

And then, there was a Neem tree. It stood a little distance away from everyone. Its roots had loosened the neat, cemented floor. I paused there, next to the roots. There are no butterflies, I thought oddly. So many units of time had passed, that in remembering solely *can't breathe can't breathe*, I had forgotten about the Pioneer I saw before leaving home.

But under the tree, I remembered again. It was cool there, a little bouquet of cold in the sweltering April second wave. 'Don't stand under trees at night. They give out carbon dioxide.' My father's rich baritone popped up in my mind, a silvery swirl inside the Covid brain fog. But how can it be any worse than *can't breathe* at any time? I asked. I must stand here. The tree seemed to be an old person, a king to the florid queen near my kitchen. I was not supposed to touch anything, except food. Of course, I stretched through the carbon dioxide of my father's concern and touched the tree bark. There were rivets and rivers running down its worried shaft. A tree that had seen more tears than usual, standing crowned in a place of death. At my feet lay a profusion of flowers – not an embarrassment of generosity, but a sprinkle of it. Not as many as my tree, but enough. I picked up a flower. It was small, neat and like a star. It would be smelling of lilac. It may have been visited by a Brown-headed barbet, *Megalaima zeylanica*, during the day.

Standing there in the cloud of my Baba's concern and the guard's warning, something was happening. It was time travel. The tree had given me a moment of normalcy. A door had opened through my brain fog. It was gentle, easy, like it had always been there – the heading home of Mary Oliver's 'Wild Geese', the slow but sure tree wisdom of Sumana Roy's *How I Became a Tree*.

Every year, I monitor trees in the city. It started with the flowers. Looking at seasonal flowers every year – Palash (*Butea monosperma*), Semal (*Bombax ceiba*), Arjuna (*Terminalia arjuna*) – on big city trees had became a shortcut to birding. The tree was the centre of the universe for the satellites that revolved around it – birds, bats, butterflies, bees, wasps, day-flying moths. Lush love stories emerged on the trees. An Indian Grey hornbill, *Ocyceros birostris*, feeding his mate with Semal flower petal bits, redder than blood against his careful, yellowed casque. Rivalries rushed forward. A pair of Common myna, *Acridotheres tristis*, trying to dislodge Rose-ringed parakeets, *Psittacula krameri*, from their Neem nest hole. Irritations bristled. A Yellow paper wasp, *Polistes olivaceus*, trying to settle on a Plain tiger butterfly, *Danaus chrysippus*, already nectaring on *Terminalia arjuna* flowers. The butterfly would shake its wings imperiously, and I would feel the wind shivering on my cheeks. The rage of little things is always more interesting than that of big ones.

I remembered too the Queen tree in her florid dress, her starry flowers. In the first whispers of spring, the ends of Neem sprigs break out in pink leaves. The leaves are carefully gathered – only the pink, only the velvety, never the green, never the leathery – to be ground into a chutney that is spiced with green chillies. It is the beginning of a new year, and this is a traditional dish to mark the time – a bitter to stymie the year's challenges; not bitter enough to make you cry. In April, the Neem flowers come. They hang like cream chandelier clusters between pinnate leaves that organize themselves in green spiral patterns. And then come the butterflies, to Delhi from Western India. They keep time well, landing daily on the Neem at nine am, when the flowers are gentled by the sun. Blossom and butterfly are the same colour, cream to cream. In the stories I write in my head, I wonder if the flowers could be butterflies that stayed. The crown of the Neem shakes with butterflies in May and April – a spectacle that takes place above people's eyeline. If the butterflies were blue, this would be all over the Internet. As it is, the Pioneer, with a J mark on each forewing, is a modest-looking butterfly visiting a modest tree. It is unfair that in the respectable medicinal nature of the tree, the Neem's beauty is overlooked.

Throughout the years before Covid, I would make wildlife lists – the mischievous Coppersmith barbet pecking at Neem drupes and stuffing its beak with figs. A Red pierrot butterfly, *Talicada nyseus,* between the Pioneers, glowing a shocking red like a subterranean jewel in underground rivers of no particular hue. On a rainy day, a peacock would shake its long, colourful, giddy mess of a tail while sitting on a Neem branch – too vivid to seem real. That day the Neem was the stolid backdrop every vain star needs – a reliable relief to the gold turquoise of India's rambunctious national bird. Between a flowering Semal and a non-flowering Neem tree, I had counted seventeen bird species. In spring, the Semal blossomed. In early summer, it was the turn of the Neem to do so. Though I couldn't smell as I stood under the hospital Neem, I remembered the *feel* of the Neem-flower scent – faint, shy, lilac.

I could breathe again. One day, I would smell again too.

PALASH

It was hard to climb stairs, harder in masks. But we were back home, a quartet of warrior poets. I felt poetry climb into my limbs even as my limbs seemed to give way. I had seen people die. The first Covid-19 dead body I saw had lain in a foetal position, like leaflets curled inside a burnt seed. The bitterness of the Neem blazed in me, prosaic and cleansing. What but the Neem had saved my spirit?

In the outdoors, beyond my quarantined self, the Palash was flowering. I felt the warm blaze of the bloom – molten, orange, defiant – sizzle on the streets and forests of my mind. The Palash tree thrives in aridity and so seems to be built for the India I know – scarce of resources, resilient, and with a complicated stem that looks like it is grieving.

Palash – *the Butea monosperma* – is native to India, and it flowers in spring and early summer when much of the forest is as dry as politician's promise during Covid. In a husk-like, browned land, the tree puts forth flowers that look like licks of flames. The moniker 'flame of the forest' is local, and apt, and a sign of spring and early summer.

I could not go out to see Palash. But the Neem-door stayed open in my mind, flapping gently in my convalescence. Trees are time travel. I opened my older pictures of Palash. A year ago, in April 2020's cruel first wave, I had found one flowering Palash tree near me. A curfew lay like a blanket over the land – the only concessions in its tight weave were trips to the chemist.

Wrapped in masks and a headscarf, only my eyes were visible. In April 2020, we didn't know what we were up against. Everything was scary. Especially the invisible things – viruses, and the threat of violence against women when the cops were busy. I didn't want to be seen. The Palash had no such asinine qualms.

The tree stood like a god, radiating with orange flowers. A plant god – one that did not need the appreciation of human worshippers, one that flowered and fruited without a built shrine. It stood on a narrow base – a 2-foot strip of the central median between two busy roads. This should not have been possible – a slow-growing, jungle tree flourishing in a tiny strip of dust, eating air pollution and noise instead of fresh dew and messages from other trees. But this Covid-tree was resistance itself. I felt like I was seeing a Palash for the first time. As I watched, a Purple sunbird flew across the road to nectar on the flowers. Its purple-gold iridescence seemed very far from washed-out blues of surgical masks.

In the room of my present isolation, I had stepped through time again. Something else seemed important, pricking at the leaves of memory. I was seized with some understanding I could not fully grasp. I started diving through the dates of my Palash pictures. I realized then that I had found my Covid-Palash exactly a year before my April 2021 infection. Usually, my annual Palash-flower monitoring took me to wildernesses in Delhi – to the ancient Aravalli hill range, heritage nurseries and protected city forests. I had not looked at the roads near me. But the first wave had drawn us into a tight bubble – and this drew me closer to dusty lanes near home, and to the unexpected jungle tree on a city road divider.

Things of personal meaning can often be little coincidences, silly for others, but invaluable flag posts for the self as we make our way through a pitiless world. A cruel universe that nevertheless has Covid-trees of Neem and Palash growing in places of death and dust; and thus, a world that still has wonder.

My little Neem and Palash discoveries gleamed in my ragged chest. One day, I would smell again, climb stairs again, and fully breathe again. One day, the masks would come off and I would be fully visible.

COVID-TREES

The Covid-trees stayed with me through 2021. The world collapsed around us, and then re-erected itself – tidal surges of sickness during a changed climate. Oxygen was on the black market – that thing we get below big trees suddenly the most commodified product in India. We learnt new words, as fierce and raging as forest fires. Oxygen concentrators. Black fungus. White fungus. RT PCR. Co-morbidities. HR CT.

CITY OF COVID-TREES

I read the paper every day to see how many more people had died. In the parking lot of a hospital, a senior official had died of Covid while waiting for a bed. Down the road, my friend's grandmother succumbed, quietly and with no complaint. A conservative right-winger I had always avoided collapsed in his drawing room, never to wake. The hospitals and their approach roads were overflowing. So was the holy Ganga river, where people threw unburnt bodies of the deceased.

There wasn't enough wood to burn the corpses. Towards the end of the April of my infection, after three consecutive days of 300 people dying in Delhi every day, the Mayor of North Delhi wrote to the Chief Minister asking that the forest department be directed to provide wood for pyres.

It was a utilitarian request – turning to the city's forests for more wood, and not to better wood chain supplies. When people were dropping like flies, would there be any hope for trees without votes? Meanwhile, parks had been converted to crematoriums, and metal pyres had melted from overuse. On WhatsApp, government propaganda was chanted by the middle class – don't talk about death, talk about the living; don't politicise, don't criticize.

But I was full of criticism. Which trees will go first, I asked myself, the Neem-door in my heart banging furiously on its imperiled frame. Would it be the Neem that stands in a hospital complex, with its flowers trampled underfoot on life-saving missions? Or that vague tree on the central median, standing amidst passing cars, with no hopes of its pods germinating on tarmac?

A positive country of grief rolled in me. The country had hills and gorges and places of rest, but the grief blazed like a sun in the sky – always following me, always touching me. In the failure of a blustering government and the false pride of the middle class, we couldn't see what was most important – a healthy environment outside our own doors.

Apart from the birds, I had also seen urban trees for how they touched lives of people. Poor families would shelter under them in the April heat. A barber would set up his little world, razors gleaming and picking up leaf reflections, his leather-backed chair looking at the world with a stiff upper lip from the deep shade. A woman would sell Jamun fruit. Beggar children would rest. All of these little units were temporarily off the streets because of the lockdown, but despite how endlessly it stretched on, the pandemic wouldn't last forever. One day, those people would need to return to their little ellipses of relief – the shade and windbreak of a mature city tree. The Indian Ministry of Earth Sciences predicts more heatwaves in India, as climate change well and truly squats amidst us. Trees will not just be playing a central role in evapotranspiration but also in providing fresh air in places whose Air Quality Index is often above 700. They will also be making the body of the city habitable, an inch closer to being tolerable in Aprils when the mercury begins to soar.

By the end of 2021, more than 4,800,000 people had died in India of Covid. None of the deaths had sunk in yet – not the single death of a thirty-four-year-old friend, nor the number of zeros in the hundreds of thousands of people dying. But another statistic pricked at me. In the last thirteen years, 112,169 trees had been felled in Delhi. Even as the pandemic raged, a 'beautification' project was taking place in the ceremonial heart of New Delhi. Workers tore down, dug and built while full ambulances trundled past. This was the Central Vista project, redeveloping India Gate, the Parliament of India, and the vistas that surrounded the buildings. Amongst these were old fruit-bearing Jamun trees. The Jamun tree gets its name from 'Jamun', a dense purple fruit that is a personal favourite only because it's a monsoon yield that lasts about fifteen days a year. This tree, the *Syzygium cumini,* throws down a dense shade, giving it the local moniker of 'AC tree'.

The Central Vista project is pegged as a redevelopment project, but it's hard to 'redevelop' a mature tree. It will cut trees, make new buildings, and create newer open spaces from the existing open spaces. It is also pegged as a nationalistic project, but does not consider the patriotism of keeping trees standing. Enraged by the cutting down of trees in the heart of the city, citizens moved the Supreme Court of India against it.

The resulting judgement calmly goes against dendrology. It suggests the translocation and replantation of mature, rooted trees.

'Currently, there are 250 & 333 trees on plot 116 and 118 respectively. 233 trees will be transplanted from Plot 118,' the government said on affidavit to the Court.

Plot number 116 holds the Parliament of India. This is a Place, an important one. But Parliament's trees are a place too, those columns of fresh air and relief, those pillars of ecological democracy.

The government then added another sparkler to its arguments in Court – the ease of replacing an old tree with a new sapling. 'And after planting additional 290 trees (including some which will be replanted) total 390 trees will be present at Plot 118. Thus, [a] total [of] 57 trees will be increased at site even after expansion.'

The final Supreme Court order allowed the Central Vista project to continue, hinged at least partly on the idea that trees are moveable, and replaceable. It seemed ironic to me that the fate of trees was being decided in buildings, and for buildings.

CITY OF COVID-TREES

In 2021, the Covid-trees in my chest were at risk of becoming pandemic pyre-wood, but in 2022, beyond the pandemic, city trees are *always* at risk from warped ideas of development and public interest. My Covid-Neem is not replaceable. My Covid-Palash is not moveable. Trees are mobile, but only through the assistance of birds, wind, bats and hands that carry seeds. A transplantation of a grown tree is a violent act; and in a dry city like Delhi, it is also a futile, fatal act. It is the drought and extinction of common good sense.

We need trees where we are. We need the trees that are to remain where they are. It is possible that city trees standing at isolated places do not have roots touching each other or fungal networks to help each other. They often live and grow socially distanced from their kin. Yet I wonder if we can be the friendly network for the tree, and if we can break more concrete so more trees can have roots touching for wood webs. The trees we choose to plant, to savour and root are important and should be the product of choice. A decolonized choice. They should be the trees of India, trees of the dust, those with complicated barks knotted both with grief and the ease of being able to withstand the North Indian summer.

I note I do not know which trees will be 'redeveloped' around the Central Vista. Will it be a respectable Neem or an AC Jamun, perhaps a slow Palash? In tree plantations around the city (and indeed many cities), the Palash is unfavoured because it is too bent, the Jamun has roots too deep for buildings with basements, and the Neem and Semal fling down too much fruit. What is favoured is beautiful and undemanding – foreign, shallow-rooted and fast-growing trees. The Queen palm, *Syagrus romanzoffiana*, making Dubai out of Delhi. The uncomplaining *Plumeria obtusa*, flowering throughout the year but shunned by local fauna. The *Tecoma stans*, more shrub than tree. The exotic, pretty Gulmohar, *Delonix regia*, horticulturally sound but ecologically empty.

I realize all trees are not equal. But another realization also touches me, as green as a Brown-headed barbet's wing feather. Covid has torn us apart, but it can also be an opportunity for a new kind of redevelopment to take root – a camaraderie with nature. With each patient having one Covid-tree for herself. We start and end our life with flowers – at birth, at deaths. We might also remember to live our life through flowers that are above our eyelines but already in our ecological memories – those of native trees.

The Neem-door swings open. I imagine a world recovered from Covid. It is a decarbonized world, and a decolonized one. Native trees grow and are grown, where people are, and where people go. Citizens are seen, and so are the trees. The concrete around trees is wilfully de-concretised. There is instead, a rootedness, a connectedness to trees, and their non-human citizens. Birdsong replaces ambulance calls. Every person has a Covid-tree; the tree-door in her heart is wide open. *Can't breathe* becomes can breathe in the shade of the AC tree and in the knowledge that seeds will be watered.

This is the city of recovery trees, and all are welcome.

ENDNOTES

Q IS FOR GARDEN

1. https://www.spiceography.com/lemon-verbena/ and S Gattuso, C M. van Baren, A Gil, A Bandoni, G Ferraro, M Gatuso, 'Morpho-histological and quantitative parameters in the characterization of lemon verbena (Aloysia citriodora palau) from Argentina', *Boletín Latinoamericano y del Caribe de Plantas Medicinales y Aromáticas*, 2008, 7 (4), 190–8, p.191 https://www.redalyc.org/pdf/856/85670402.pdf.

2. 'The woke National Trust risks trivialising our rich history; It is an act of modern narcissism to treat the past as if it were the present.' *Telegraph* Online, 26 Oct. 2020, p. NA. Gale OneFile: News, https://link.gale.com/apps/doc/A639483196/STND?u=rdg&sid=STND&xid=f567e22d. Accessed 6 Nov. 2020.

3. Thank you So Mayer for this brilliant image.

4. Some digitised images from the Radev Collection are available via Bridgeman Images: https://www.bridgemanimages.co.uk/en/collections/RADEV-COLLECTION.

5. Eliott Kennerson, 'Everything You Never Wanted to Know About Snail Sex', 14 March 2017, https://www.kqed.org/science/1446777/everything-you-never-wanted-to-know-about-snail-sex.

6. *House and Garden*, 'From the archive: Vita Sackville-West on her garden at Sissinghurst (1950)', 20 May 2020, https://www.houseandgarden.co.uk/article/from-the-archive-vita-sackville-west-on-her-garden-at-sissinghurst.

THE LAST FLIGHT OF THE GOSHAWK?

1. *The Silk Roads – A New History of the World*, Peter Frankopan. Bloomsbury, 2015.

ENDNOTES

2. *New English Canaan* by Thomas Morton of Merrymount, Jack Dempsey 2000, Digital Scanning Inc.

3. Ibid

4. Ibid

5. Rabbit haemorrhagic disease – Wikipedia *see also* New 'viral cocktail' killing hares in UK and Ireland, scientist warns | Wildlife | *The Guardian see also* Rabbit Haemorrhagic Disease - an overview | ScienceDirect Topics see also Rabbit-killing virus may have mutated to kill hares too | *New Scientist see also* Burying pet rabbits in gardens could spread deadly virus, vets warn | Pets | *The Guardian*

6. *Finding Balance – The Genealogy of Massasoit's People and the Oral & Writing History of the Seaconke Pokanoket Wampanoag Tribal Nation,* Deborah Spears Moorhead. Blue Hand Books, Massachusetts, 2014

7. Department for Environment, Food and Rural Affairs Animal & Plant Health Agency Advice Services Team – International Disease Monitoring 1 Updated Outbreak Assessment #25 Highly pathogenic avian influenza (HPAI) in the UK, and Europe 12 August 2021 Ref: VITT/1200 HPAI in the UK and Europe.

8. Dozens of swans die in Stratford upon Avon bird flu outbreak. BBC News. *see also* Avian influenza in wild birds: 2021, GOV.UK (publishing.service.gov.uk)

9. Avian influenza in wild birds: 2021, GOV.UK (publishing.service.gov.uk)

10. This figure was supplied to me by a senior member of the British Falconers Club and rests on the correct definition of a falconer. This is as specific as it was since the nomadic Mongols invented it. Falconry is the use of trained indigenous raptor to seasonally hunt indigenous wild quarry to feed the raptor or human. Anything outside this definition owes more to the mindset of exotic bird keeping and elaborate rare breeds than a global falconry heritage.

11. Falconry, a living human heritage – intangible heritage, Culture Sector, UNESCO

ENDNOTES

12. Avian influenza (who.int) *see also* Factory farms of disease: how industrial chicken production is breeding the next pandemic | Global health | The Guardian.

NONE OF THIS SHOULD BE HERE

1. 'Beyond the town, the only transition between the Strip and the Mojave Desert is a zone of rusting beer cans' is from Robert Venturi, Denise Scott Brown and Stephen Izenour, *Learning From Las Vegas*, The MIT Press, 1977. Page 35.

2. In H. L. Mencken's words that there exists in America, a 'lust for the hideous, the delight in ugliness for its own sake' is quoted in William Least Heat-Moon's *Blue Highways: A Journey Into America.* Picador with Secker & Warburg, 1984. Page 357.

3. This fact is on page 5 of an article by Gabu Heindl in the *Journal of Architectural Education* (1984-), November 2005, vol. 59, no. 2, pp. 5–12, Taylor & Francis, Ltd. on Behalf of The Association of Collegiate Schools of Architecture.

4. Article quoted is by Blake Apgar, 'New Golf Courses Can't Use Colorado River Water, Las Vegas Board Says', 2 November 2021 and updated 3 November 2021 from the *Las Vegas Review–Journal.* www.reviewjournal.com/news/politics-and-government/clark-county/new-golf-courses-cant-use-colorado-river-water-las-vegas-board-says-2470511/

5. Ian Zabarte, Principal Man of The Western Bands of The Shoshone Nation of Indians, is quoted in his article 'A Message From The Most Bombed Nation On Earth' in *Al Jazeera*, 29 August 2020.

6. The fact that the bomb dropped on Hiroshima in 1945 created 13 kilotonnes of nuclear fallout; whereas between 1951 and 1992 nuclear testing on Shoshone land created 620 kilotonnes is quoted by Zabarte from a 2009 study in the *Nevada Law Journal.* Published in the above *Al Jazeera* article.

ENDNOTES

7. The final quote from Ian Zabarte is also from the above *Al Jazeera* article.

8. An article titled '4,300 Sheep Near Nevada Nuclear Tests Died in '53' dating from 15 February 1979 (section A, page 15) was retrieved from *The New York Times* online archives. www.nytimes.com/1979/02/15/archives/4300-sheep-near-nevada-nuclear-tests-died-in-53-a-will-ful-refusal.html

9. From William Least Heat-Moon's *Blue Highways*. Page 149.

10. Some of the discussion around the burial of nuclear waste in the West is from an article by William Beaver, 'The Demise of Yucca Mountain', in *The Independent Review*, Spring 2010, vol. 14, no. 4 (Spring 2010), Pp. 535–547. Published by the Independent Institute.

11. From the arch out loud website at: www.archoutloud.com/nuclear-results.html

12. From the 'Preserve and Transmit Memory' page at the Andra website: www.andra.fr/nos-expertises/conserver-et-transmettre-la-memoire

13. The thoughts and quotes from Aldo Leopold are from his chapter 'The Land Ethic' from A Sand County Almanac, Penguin Random House, 1949. Pages 155–173.

14. This quote is from Simone de Beauvoir's America Day by Day based on the author's trip to the United States in 1947. First published in 1954 as *L'Amérique au jour le jour* by Editions Gallimard. This quote is from the 1998 Victor Gollancz edition. Page 380. Translated by Carol Cosman.

THE JUDGES

KATHRYN AALTO is an American historian, teacher and author living in England. Her books include the *New York Times* bestseller *The Natural World of Winnie-the-Pooh: A Walk Through the Forest that Inspired the Hundred Acre Wood* (2015), and *Writing Wild: Women Poets, Ramblers and Mavericks Who Shape How We See the Natural World* (2020). She contributes to several publications and co-founded the Rural Writing Institute.

ELIZABETH-JANE BURNETT is an author and academic whose work has a largely environmental focus. Her publications include a *Sunday Times* Poetry Book of the Year, *Swims* (2017) and a nature writing memoir, *The Grassling* (2019), a winner of the Penguin Random House WriteNow award. She is Associate Professor in Creative Writing at Northumbria University.

MATTHEW COBB is Professor of Zoology at the University of Manchester, where his research focuses on the sense of smell, insect behaviour and the history of science. He is the author of popular science books including *The Idea of the Brain* (shortlisted for the 2020 Baillie Gifford Prize) and *The Genetic Age: Our Perilous Quest to Edit Life*.

THE JUDGES

SARA HUNT (CHAIR) worked in publishing in London and New York before founding award-winning independent press Saraband in 1994, specialising in nature, place and life writing, as well as literary fiction. She has published award-nominated and winning titles in prizes ranging from the Booker, Wainwright and Rathbones Folio prizes to the Lakeland and Highland awards.

WILL SMITH is a bookseller at Grasmere's Sam Read's, paperback previewer for *The Bookseller* magazine, and an academic with a doctorate in Canadian Literature whose book reviews also feature monthly in *Cumbria Life* and on BBC Radio Cumbria. He has co-edited a poetry anthology, *Companions of Nature*, and Lakeland Book Award-winning *Grasmere: a History in 55½ Buildings*. He was a judge of the 2019 Costa Book Awards.

ACKNOWLEDGEMENTS

The Nature Chronicles Prize co-founders, Emma Dickens and Rebecca Scott, would like to thank the following for their wise counsel, enthusiasm and support from the outset and/or at key moments:

Simon Appleby at Bookswarm, Christine Brock, Natasha Carthew, Kim Kremer at Notting Hill Editions, Kate Murrell, Jamie Normington at Cumbria Wildlife Trust, James Rebanks, Paul Scully and everyone at the Kendal Mountain Book Festival.

Thank you also to all the readers and judges, and first and foremost, to those who entered this, our inaugural prize. It was an immense privilege to read your careful, candid, heartfelt work.